FINDING SIERRA

A JOURNEY TO A BETTER ME, THE ONLY WAY OUT IS IN

GW00758574

SIERRA CLARK

First published by Ultimate World Publishing 2021
Copyright © 2021 Sierra Clark

ISBN

Paperback: 978-1-922497-90-1
Ebook: 978-1-922497-91-8

Sierra Clark has asserted her rights under the Copyright, Designs and Patents Act 1988 to be identified as the author of this work. The information in this book is based on the author's experiences and opinions. The publisher specifically disclaims responsibility for any adverse consequences which may result from use of the information contained herein. Permission to use information has been sought by the author. Any breaches will be rectified in further editions of the book.

Cover design: Ultimate World Publishing
Layout and typesetting: Ultimate World Publishing
Editor: Rebecca Low
Cover photo: AlenaMorgana-Shutterstock.com

Ultimate World Publishing
Diamond Creek,
Victoria Australia 3089
www.writeabook.com.au

Dedications

To the Hugh D. Burgess estate, to every black child knowing who they are, who they really are! To the embellishment of systemic racism and every life taken. To not being judged by the color of their skin, instead by the content of their character.

To no longer needing hashtags like #BlackLivesMatter, #CancerSucks and #NotMySon. To Black Wall Street Part II.

To the freedom bells that have yet to ring, to the unheard cries of our ancestors whose scarred and unscarred backs we stand upon.

To my mother, father, siblings and all my fill in the blank people. And last but not least, to my legacy, and generational wealth.

Contents

Dedications iii

Foreword vii

Testimonials 1

Bio 5

About the Author 7

Introduction 9

Chapter 1: ♥ Joyful Everything ♥ 13

Chapter 2: ∞ Identity Crisis ∞ 37

Chapter 3: ♥ Tables Turn ♥ 59

Chapter 4: ∞ I Am Not Your Mother ∞ 81

Chapter 5: ♥ Adult Life ♥ 93

Chapter 6: ∞ Spreading My Wings ∞ 101

Chapter 7: ♥ You Didn't Put in on This ♥ 113

Chapter 8: ∞ "40" I'm Coming Out ∞ 121

Chapter 9: ♥ Self Planting Seeds ♥ 131

Chapter 10: ∞ D. A. R. E 2 Be ∞ 139

Behind the Pages 145

Stepping Over Fear 146

D.A.R.E 2 B 147

Disclaimer 151

Afterword 153

Call to action 155

Speaker Bio 157

Foreword

Greetings, this foreword is an honor for me to write. I have known Sierra for quite some time, but we never actually physically made contact. I remember the first time Sierra popped up on my social media newsfeed. She had this encouraging line she used to always say, "A better you equals a better me."

I have my own way of expressing this same statement in various ways, but Ms. Clark came out of nowhere and dropped this defining line on my followers and me, and it has stuck with me for at least the last three and a half to four years. I began to research Ms. Clark only to find out that she was a female evangelist/pastor. I was intrigued by her spirit and energy even before physically meeting and getting to know her.

I think finding the courage to travel on a journey to acquire knowledge of self is one that is always underestimated. We love to tell people that you have to gain knowledge of themselves, but we never give them the tools to make sure that they can defend themselves while they are on that journey. Tools that can help them nurture themselves while on this journey

The journey to the enlightenment of self is a long, hard, lonely, and sometimes depressing journey. And the majority of the time, you'll be on this journey by yourself, for yourself. You will lose a lot of weight, and I mean weight as in individuals in your life.

Now, this book is not only an insight into things that Ms. Clark had to journey back through and face to regain the essence of who she is, her most authentic self. This book is good for the reader also because it shows that no matter what you are going through in life, no matter what level of life you are living, no matter what experiences are still imprinted on your inner self, it is still you who holds all the master keys to unlock all the mysteries of who you are.

As you journey through this book and you take a ride down Sierra's memory lane, let this book be a book of encouragement, a book of revelations, and a book of enlightenment. Because everyone's story is different, it's still your story, and only you can tell it. So, no matter how this book either feeds you, or encourages you, know that it did all that for her as well.

As I have watched Ms. Clark on her journey for the last year and a half, almost two years, she has come out of a stage in her life in which she was trying to regain who she is without losing who she has become. It's moments like this that define us, that also break us. But, the true defining moment is when you can no longer be broken.

The truest defining moment is when you begin to look at those cracks, all those breaks, and all those scars and see the beauty in it. You see the luster and shine in it, and you see the power in it. Now those scars, those bruises, those cracks in your character, and the things that set you apart from the rest of the crowd are your battle scars, your stripes in the field of life.

You are now ready to allow her scars, to allow her recollection of those moments in her life, and her personality give you the courage to walk down your own path. Allow her words, experiences, ups and downs, losses, and accomplishments to become your artillery and weapon in life.

Let that weapon in your life hold you down and support you as you walk this journey of self-enlightenment and self-knowledge. So, as she has grown, as she has gained confidence in who she is, as she has realized that she has always been the key factor in all decisions, situations and obstacles in life, Sierra has learned that it was by choice that those things were allowed in her life. Through realizing that, she knows that the power of choice is a hard one, and you have to be intentional with yourself.

I've been a great friend and a teacher, but I have also been a student. I have also reciprocated through her love, her spirit, her frequency and her power. These are things that we all have. These are things that we are not taught or don't get to experience until later in life. But, the later in life moments are by design.

You have to go through the storm in order to see the true beauty of the stars. Remember, even a plane starts on the ground and even at its peak of altitude, there is still turbulence in the ride. So, as you, too, rise above your storm clouds and clear the trees, you'll experience the turbulence of living and experiencing who you truly are. But, don't allow the limbs to block your sight or the wind to hold you back

My name is Tim Barber. I'm a student of metaphysics and all things needed to prepare for the journey of self-learning. I believe that the power that lies at the core of self is buried beneath all the layers the subconscious has formed to protect us.

I like to get people to look back on their lives, even in dark moments, and find themselves. When looking back on our lives, we tend to find strength and forgotten gifts. Now, a lot of truth comes with heartbreaking effects, and a lot of gifts come with the realization that you may have been outcasted or overlooked. But, in the in-depth evaluation of self, you will discover your entire self. As a whole is the only way you can truly evolve.

As an entire entity, being unified is where you unlock untapped potential and true knowledge of self. Without going back to reconnect with the inner child, the adolescent you, and the current version of you, how are you truly gaining the full spectrum of self? These phases are key in your evolution.

The inner child has to be rekindled and embraced. Whatever experiences you encountered that traumatized you, uplifted you, or even if you simply had a boring childhood, these are experiences you have to recall. See, our true magical selves lie within the happiness and security of the child. Once there, take time to give them a voice, and make time to listen to their voice.

The child is the first and the original God-mind. The creator and architect of who you are and all the personalities you have channeled. Through the child's experiences, it formulated the necessary energy to protect itself from whatever or whoever it deemed a threat. It was the experiences that brought forth a protector, a comedian, and a fighter. The intelligent one and even the nurturer. But, we aren't made aware of these things, so we don't realize it has occurred in this fashion.

Then, you have an adolescent or teenager. The one they love to label rebellious or the wonderer. Recall the inner child and its capacity to create without losing itself inside its own creation. So, the adolescent is the combination of the child's best creations, whether it's the humor, the strength, the introvert, the nurturer, the leader, or even the protector. Who you choose to walk into your adolescence as is your inner child's choice.

But again, you have to go back and look at how you walk through those times. What moments solidified or broke the character or characters that you were? You need to be able to see these moments in HD and hear them in Dolby Digital surround sound in order to raise yourself out of whatever dark corner you left remnants of yourself in.

Those pieces that were chipped away by life are pieces we can't leave behind. You have to go back with your spiritual broom and your mental dustpan and clean up the mess you thought you were. Don't forget to allow yourself time to embrace and indulge in the many waves of emotions. These are also keys to sustaining your growth. Learn from what you feel, so you won't be afraid or crippled by these emotions later on in your journey.

Allow them to empower you where they once may have made you seem weak or vulnerable. Allow the insecurities of your past teach you how to strengthen yourself now. As you emerge into the adolescent essence of self, don't be hesitant to feel. To heal, you have to feel.

This version of you was probably the most confused when it came to emotions. But, this is where you either discovered the immense pressure of those emotions or the power they possess. So, as you embark on this journey within and reconnect, be direct with yourself. Direct with what you can recall.

Write down with intent the memories, write the details of your environment, the people, the colors that come, and even the smells. Your senses play a vital role in this process. Sight, sounds, and smell, the three S's. Remember that.

Now, your current self, the great work of art the human experience has created. Is this you, your best you? Are you really living your best life? I would bet my money on no. Simply due to the natural fact that if you're reading this book, like Sierra, this in-depth journey is new to you also, which is actually great.

You, too, can now take the power that has always been in you and truly use it at its full potential. Now you know a few easy steps to take as you embark on this journey.

Be kind to yourself. Listen to yourself, and really spend time with all of you.

Timothy Barber

September 17, 2020

Testimonials

I've known Sierra Clark for 12 years. We have been through a lot in our friendship; I watched her move through different stages in life. I remember us going out in Downtown St. Pete and dancing the night away. I can recall Sierra always supporting her family and always carrying everyone's weight on her shoulders, even if that meant working overtime to get it all done. I recall the spiritual journey Sierra was on, connecting with herself. She always had scripture and symbols, written in chalk, all over her dashboard in her car. She knew I never understood it, but it was her growth, and however she needed to find happiness was alright with me.

Sierra always gave great advice, and she was a great listener. But, as we know, it's hard to listen to that great advice and practice what you preach in our own real-life situations. I would always tell her, "Please just be mean, snap just one time, stop letting people run over you and use you, girl. No matter who they are!" Her key thing to do is smile that beautiful smile and say, "It's okay, Boo." We call each other Boo. She always looks at the sunny side of everything and remains optimistic. God loves a heart as big as that, and it will get rewarded. I still wanted her to pop off.

She never judged anyone; no matter how big the issue or secret may have been, she is a forgiver. I always wanted her to want the best for her too. It just frustrated me because she could tell me what I deserved but did not know what she deserved. My friend was such a lover and a giver. We would be out to eat, and she would make sure to engage with the server and always made sure to ask them how they were feeling. That's just one example of how she used to go above and beyond to love on people.

She is truly a queen and deserves so much more than she was accepting from people who didn't appreciate her. Sierra always spoke of love in the light of rainbows and butterflies, and that's what she deserved. I was there through the journey of her divorcing her husband, which is when I saw the big change. This is when Finding Sierra Clark really started to unfold. I watched her hurt while even questioning herself. But then she did a 360. She bossed up and started working on her, a full makeover, changing herself, and changing her financial situation.

She became more independent and focused on advancing herself in her career path. She began to focus on her education and figure out what she wanted out of life. She stopped hiding behind the greatness of others. I have listened to her confront the ones who hurt her, and let me tell you, the quiet girl definitely has a voice, and it's beautiful, powerful, and strong.

I see her finally loving Sierra's nakedness. Sierra's growth from 2010 to 2020 has been drastic but well-paced, and she is more confident in who she is. I love you always sis, happy I know you, and I am so proud of the woman I see you have grown into. Go girl, strut your stuff!

I saw her grow from Sierra to Marie-rie. Sierra is a true friend indeed. Even after becoming Marie-rie , that has not changed, but there is a difference between the two. Now, if I may tell you about my friend Sierra who took on shit and carried the weight of everybody else, putting them first. This was later the very thing that broke her down.

Now, don't get me wrong, Sierra at times could muster up a lil attitude from time to time, especially if she felt like she was backed into a corner. But deep down, the little person I called Marie-rie just wasn't ready to come out. Sierra was always like Bob the Builder when it came to loving people. Instead of allowing everybody else to carry their own weight and clean up their own mess, she would do it.

Marie-rie, that's my chick, she's family.

This chick Marie-rie is outspoken, cares about others' feelings, but then again, doesn't, if that makes sense? Marie-rie, I must say, has earned her gangster card and her crown to become the goon who loves herself before anyone else. Marie-rie is my chick, my homie, my buddy, and more. So, to you, she's Sierra, but to me, she's Marie-rie.

Bio

Sierra is a woman of many talents and has a gift that allows her to see through dirt and despair and still see the light and love in everything. She has been a mentor for the majority of her life, dating back to even her childhood days. Her connection with her community comes from her relationship with her elders as well as the babies

Sierra is a descendant of a Honduran-born grandfather. The daughter of Leroy Clark and Eliza Burgess. She's a sister to five girls and two brothers. With intention, she uses her life for love to light to others. One of Sierra Clark's superpowers is love. She knows that she's created to love and build others up. She calls this loving on people.

Allowing her light to shine is an intentional characteristic about her. Since 2013, she has been an active member of the Pinellas County mentoring program. It's her way of giving back and paying it forward. She currently volunteers at three public schools in Pinellas County by mentoring youth in all aspects.

Although she has no children of her own, she takes great joy in being a part of the village it takes to raise a child that her loved ones entrust her to be a part of.

She is a proud member of Manifest University, an online community, tribe, and family. She's worked at the local children's hospital for the past 14 plus years.

About the Author

I'm Sierra Clark, a native of Saint Petersburg, Florida. Creator of Hearts Talk podcast and founder of It's A Heart Thang LLC.

When I'm not on the air or working on creating multiple streams of income, I'm doing heart thangs, loving on people. Rather, the loving is done directly in something I can do, hence why I've been in the healthcare field off and on for 22 years. Or, I focus on loving indirectly by pointing them in the right direction or helping to bring balance and clarity in themselves.

I am spiritually aware I bring love to this planet. Mentally, I know there is more to this world than the words written in red. Physically, I understand that I am a beacon of light for others.

I've always been enthusiastic about other's growth and success. I love when others are awakened to the beauty in themselves.

Now, I can also see the beauty inside myself and my purpose in this experience of life.

Introduction

I've decided it is time to step over fear! It's time to see it for the illusion it was. It's time that I got out of my way and stopped hindering myself from living the life that leads me to my destiny. I started to be intentional about our decisions by checking things twice, even down to who we allow into our space. This was going to be vital as I had to get to know myself again. Hell, it was a "allow me to reintroduce myself" kind of moment.

The gavel has hit the bench, and we are calling **"Order in The Court!"**

I'm writing this book because I've been on a journey to find My Best, Most Magical Self. My story will help those who are looking to become their authentic self. This book needed to be written because it's time we all get out of our way and stop hindering ourselves from living a life that leads to our destiny.

Let's start from the beginning, from the ground floor. I had to go back to my roots. Not only was I going to have to take a journey within, but I was also instructed that my healing, and some answers that I seek, was going to come from people, places, and things. So, we started to pay attention a lot more to the little things. Feeling out our surroundings.

❤ *The Good Bad and Ugly* ❤

Life is filled with disappointment. In intense times of suffering, I know I can be tempted to blame myself. I haven't let you down; my promises will prevail in every problem you face.

When doubt overcomes your faith, stirring up despair and bitterness, call upon me and seek my presence. Come to me with a humble, submissive attitude, an honor in the midst of adversity. The way you respond to disappointment has an enormous impact on the outcome of your troubles.

Don't listen to the enemy. Don't believe the lies. I am with you to deliver you. I am merciful, full of love, and eager to pour out my grace into your life. Don't always take your troubles at face value; I have ways of working within them to go beyond your comprehension. I have a plan for you that goes far beyond all you could hope for or imagine. So, don't be surprised by setbacks. In this world, you will have trouble, but victory is always assured when you trust in me completely, accepting the good and the bad, living and hoping through faith.

> "We accept the good that God gives us.
> Shouldn't we also accept the bad?"
>
> **JOB 2:10**

CHAPTER 1

♥ Joyful Everything ♥

I was so ready for bed that it felt like I did a high jump up our 18-step, L-shaped staircase. Once my feet touched the top, I beelined to my bedroom to call it a night. I smiled at this very thought throughout the day, so I already knew that it was going to be an early night. Suddenly, there was an urge for me to go into the guest bedroom. Well, my quiet space is what I was currently using it as. Since we hardly ever had guests over, I called this room the lighthouse room. I've collected lighthouses over the past 20 years once I learned the story behind them and their purpose. They were always symbolic to me of never feeling or being lost.

I'll always be able to find my way back home.

The two main purposes for a lighthouse are to serve as a navigational aid and to warn boats of dangerous areas. It's like a traffic sign on the sea. Decorating this room was so exciting for me. I could finally take all these lighthouses I had collected and give them a place to live. I felt like I was putting down an internal weight.

I mean, this was a serious thing for me too. People even bought me lighthouse things for my birthdays and holidays. I finally moved into a big enough space; actually, this space was my gift from my husband Greg as my first-anniversary gift. We had closed on our three-bedroom, two and a half bath home on August 24th, four days after our first-anniversary celebration. This gave me more than enough space where I could actually dedicate a room to all my lighthouse stuff. I could cry just thinking about what decorating this room meant to me as I unpacked the boxes and unwrapped the bubble wrap from certain things.

Hanging lighthouse pictures was an inward victory because I finally felt like we were home, and we would never be lost at the sea of our own thoughts or our own self ever again. My favorite lighthouse was a gift from Ms. Land and Auntie Tam. It was very nice, heavy, and made of ceramic. It took batteries and had a rotating light like an actual lighthouse, and when it was on, it lit up the whole room.

So, I used the room as my quiet space since I knew we would not have a lot of company over. I made this my meditation space for writing in my journal and reading my devotional. I never needed an excuse to go inside this room, so I welcomed the idea of going in that day. Never thinking anything strange about the small, still voice that rerouted me. Also, I don't think I had read it in a few days, so the excitement of my new destination made me forget about just how sleepy I was.

The request to go read my journal didn't feel strange or come with any warning signs. I sat on the side of the bed because my journal lived on the nightstand. I took my time reading the words, probably not soaking them in like I definitely would do when it's morning time, and I'm about to start my day. Nevertheless, I had completed the task. There was definitely a sereneness about this room that you could just feel. I found myself waking up later; it seemed I had dozed off, and I wasn't sure for how long. So, I decided to go get into bed with my husband.

Although, I knew I would sleep better in my quiet space because that mattress we spent so much money on made my back hurt. But, if he was in there and not sleeping on the couch, then I'd sleep in the bed with him. It no longer felt like I was walking but gliding along. I'm sure it had to do with a combination of me being sleepy and being overcome with the peace I felt when leaving the lighthouse room.

Now that I write about it, it definitely sounds like the side effects of being under anesthesia. Stopping in the master bathroom for my nighttime ritual of washing my face, brushing my teeth, and then peeing, I could hear the whispers of my bed calling my name, and I remember seeing Gregory standing on his side of the bed. I was mentally trying to get my strength together to jump up into the bed. I heard the shaky sound of Gregory's words as I tuned in to make out what he was saying, the echo of his words pushed through.

"We need to talk."

The words rang like bells in my eardrums, sending a shock through me like that of a defibrillator when trying to revive a person. My heart dropped, and I said ok as I slid down the side of the bed onto the floor and listened to him talk. He said that he no longer wanted to be married. Well, his exact words were, he was unsure if we should have gotten married. I blacked out, perhaps the anesthesia had kicked in. I could still hear him talking faintly like he was now far away, repeating the same thing over and over, just in different ways.

I remember saying to him, "Does this mean you want a divorce?"

He said, "No, I'm just unsure."

Since I was sitting on the floor, he couldn't see me because we had a high bed that was set up off the ground with a very thick mattress. I was then comforted from this wave of emotion, although my heart started beating fast, and my hands began to sweat. I think I even recall wiping a tear from my cheek. The last words I read from my devotional just moments before replayed over in my head. **"We accept the good that God gives, shouldn't we accept the bad?" dated February 13th, 2017.**

There was that numbness again; it had been some years since I had to deal with it, or more like since it haunted me. I'll never forget that feeling, but there it was, wrapping itself around me like the tight hug you get when you are happy to see an old friend. I repeated to myself slowly as if coming out of a daze or, better yet, waking up from a bad dream. I'm not sure if we should've gotten married, he said.

Those words answered what my female intuition had felt four months ago. In October, around my birthday, I was concerned about my marriage, feeling like it was about to come to an end, feeling like something was wrong, feeling like there was a fire in my kitchen where I could smell the smoke, but I was unable to determine where the smoke was coming from. I mentioned all of this plus more to Gregory that night at the dinner table.

In my plea for knowing that something was happening, I could feel it. I asked questions like, "Are you happy with our marriage?" "Is there anything I can do?" "Is there anything I should not do?" Sometimes as women, we do the most, and we think that men have to settle or deal with it because we are women. I know that's not what this book is about, so I'll save that for my other book. ☺ I asked Gregory, "What can we do better to help us be stronger individually, that can grow us collectively?"

We had done post-marital counseling and premarital counseling already. I felt that we had every key needed to unlock any problem that would arise in our marriage **if we used it**. He assured me that things were ok. Like I had just made all of this up or something. The puzzled look on his face said he had no idea what I was talking about. As if these were just made up emotions.

When I was finally able to get my mouth to move, I replied to him, "You say you are unsure, but why is there something telling me that your mind is already made up?" I can't remember much more about how that night ended, like when I got up off the floor, did I cry myself to sleep? Did I ask more questions? You know, things like this.

I do remember some things about the morning. It definitely didn't start off with me lying in bed, looking up at the ceiling, going over the tasks for the day, or trying to convince myself to get out of bed and start my morning. I don't remember the sequence of events, but I do remember at some point...oh see, it's coming back to me now.

I was in the living room with Gregory and his grandparents, who were in town for his sister's wedding. I wasn't attending the wedding because I had to work. Yet, it was still nice to feel everyone's excitement. I always cried at weddings, even if they were on T.V, which Precious called me out on one day. She saw me wiping my face and asked, "Are you crying?" I replied that I always cry at weddings. Suddenly, my phone rang. It was a call from my mom (another bomb) on top of what already felt like Pearl Harbor. My mom's brother, my grandmother's oldest son, Larry, had passed away. I remember us holding hands and praying at some point before they left. Gregory and I definitely did what we always did, pretended that things were OK!

Yet, something was different this time. I was surely going through the emotions, and something was not the same. I would come to find out later, that thing was me no longer wanting to sweep things under the rug and pretend they don't exist. You see, I was passive and complacent with myself. Never listening to myself when I spoke up, always questioning myself and second-guessing.

I was never confident in my own skin, never assured in my own headspace. I had major struggles with identity issues. I felt as if it wasn't ok for anyone or myself, for that fact, to love me. The absence of my mother and father left me in a great place of uncertainty. How in the world could anybody love me when the two people that created me and gave me life didn't stay around to love me? I told myself there was no way anyone else could.

Brian Hyppolite, the author of *Manifesting You. 111 keys to unlocking your divinity*, gave me the word audacity: noun (1. ***A willingness to take bold risk* 2. *Rude or disrespectful behavior; impudence***). This book wasn't like other self-help books I've read. To make my point, I'll go out on a limb and say it was like every other self-help book written to help you. But, let's be truthful. No matter how good the intentions of the writer, nothing happens until you apply the advice.

What made this book different from the others was that it was speaking to me, let's call it divine timing. It was saying to give myself the credit I deserve. I was finally at my **ENOUGH IS ENOUGH** stage and was ready to put in the work for my self-care this time around. It was telling me, "It is time," like Mufasa told Simba in *The Lion King*. I needed to be who I needed to be for me. I was so ready for some self-application! I was now at this crossroads within, dealing with my trash, where I had been here numerous times before. I could feel my insides smiling at this audacity I had tapped into. I remembered something I had read a while back that brought me to a slower pace in going around this mountain within myself.

It's said, and I'm paraphrasing, that my parent's only job was to create me, despite the good, bad, ugly, or indifferent parts of them. They were the perfect combination that equaled the right proportion that destiny needed to create me. Marrying Gregory was another place to hide, another place to go where I knew I could be complacent with myself. At this time, I remembered the lyrics of a song that says, "There's a stranger in my house, it took a while to figure out! I have finally identified her, and ironically, she looks a lot like me." You know the saying when you point the finger, there's always three pointed back at you.

I knew this marriage would bring on some challenges and some changes that would require me to identify and let go of certain parts of me. As far back as I can remember, I've always felt disconnected. Ok, picture it like this, you take a box of puzzle pieces and dump them out on the table, and they go everywhere, some even sliding across the table onto the floor. That is how I had always felt, scattered in a bunch of different ways.

I answered to the feeling of being broken and disconnected like I did if you called my name. There's a quote that says, "It's not what they call you, but what you answer to."

I can now identify this in certain chapters of my life where there was definitely a disconnect and strong feelings of being inconsistent. I thought marriage was a place I could hide until I was put together again. I thought I had found my partner in crime, the one that was going to help me fight all my boogiemen and the parts of myself that kept getting in my way.

I thought I was in a secure place where I could finally sort through all the puzzle pieces of my identity to find exactly who and what Sierra was actually made of. I had always spent so much time giving myself away, so when I needed myself, I had nothing left to give. I remember crying on the way home from our honeymoon, internal tears, from a place I didn't know even existed. Some tears managed to seep through my eye gates.

Now I see, it all started on that flight back from the US Virgin Islands, and my spirit was just dealing with me. It was saying to me that you can't be this version of yourself and love Gregory in the way that you need to love him. It was asking me how I could properly let this love from my heart flow for him, as scripture says. How was I supposed to love if my heart was guarded was the question I kept hearing. Oh, my tears didn't stop there. I cried the whole first month of our marriage.

I felt like I was being exposed and that the rug was being pulled out from under me. I had done self-reflection before, but this time was totally different. It was happening with or without me, whether I wanted it to or not. I was being called to the center of the stage, and I was surrounded by past, present, and future versions of myself. I was dealing with what they had to say, and of course, I shared this with my husband. I had to because, oftentimes, he would come home from work and see me crying.

When we were riding in the car, he would just see the tears randomly fall from my face. This was definitely a threshing floor experience, where like the old days, they would divide the chaff from the wheat. I was definitely being divided. I felt like things were being subtracted from me, but only after I dealt with them, only after we spent time together, only after acknowledging and identifying what it was here to show me.

Pretending is what I did. I had become extremely good at it. Hell, I was making pretty little trees out of what was a bright red flag. You see, I've won a few Grammys, walked the red carpet, even showed up for my star being revealed on Broadway. I was that good at acting! We did end up getting a divorce.

When I think back, I can remember Gregory often saying to me throughout the divorce process, "Try to see the good out of this Sierra." I was like, where's the good?

JOB 2:10 **"We accept the good that God gives us. Shouldn't we accept the bad?"** To answer that, yes, you should be willing to accept all parts of your journey equally. Scripture says it this way, "All things work together for my good." There is even a phrase, **"Nothing missing, nothing broken."** Put it all together without subtracting. What do you have?

♥ *Breaking cycles* ♥

These are what we now call the steps to recovery because finding joy in those places, the good, bad, ugly, and indifferent, helped me discover different parts of myself. It was like meeting long lost parts of me. This was a real awakening. It was so real that I started talking in third, second, first, and sometimes what seemed like a fourth person. Referring to myself as, us, me, we, they, and I. The M.U.S (Made Up Stuff) was not letting me go easily. This was going to be hard, but I realized that I had fought my way through a lot of things, which was training me for a time such as this.

Since I've already experienced and survived the hard shit life had hit me with, I realized that we were at the place where we had no choice but to stand up for ourselves this time around. Finally, knowing I needed myself, I realized that I had to be my own hero. I realized that I had been consistent with so many other people while they had been inconsistent with me, and they were perfectly fine with it too. If I may give you a **WARNING**, be careful of those people that you can clearly see are alright with you being loyal and consistent with them while watching you be inconsistent with yourself.

We were at the core of ourselves, face down in the deepest parts of our inner being, and it was no doubt scary, yet it was empowering and magical all at the same time. It was full of energy, and I can't even call it a feeling because it felt like more than a feeling; it felt like destiny. This is the only way I can describe it using words. I can hear it calling to me, how do we overcome these things for good? Is there a way out of this box? How can I make sure we never do a lap around that mountain again? How do we get out of this fortified kingdom that we've built?

The same small still voice that rerouted me whispered, **THE ONLY WAY OUT, IS IN!** I didn't want to be there, yet this seemed to be a mandated journey. We were currently on empty; we had been completely freed of the old version of self. Sierra was no longer in control. I read in *Manifesting You* that if you don't master **self**, you will be **mastered by self**. I had spent 39 years being mastered by myself, and I was now changing the narrative. It was time that I took control. It was time that I told life how this game was going to be played. Those 111 keys that were placed in a book and titled *Manifesting* You helped give me the Audacity: **A willingness to take a bold risk.**

My words were being spoken with assertiveness and authority as I was talking to my friend Rochel.

"I said that from my diaphragm too."

It was time that we stood up for ourselves! It was time that we spoke up for ourselves! It was time that I saw what other people said what they were seeing in me. As I write this, I recall the times I spent in the bathroom crying during my shifts working at the nursing home. I would often get told by the residents and their families when they visited that they know how my mother and father are so proud of me. I'd smile, laugh, and agree with them, pretending just like I did when I was in elementary school. All the while, in my mind, thinking, neither one of them has any idea what I'm doing at this moment.

Sure, it's definitely rewarding when others can say how great they think you are, but it is self-empowering when you know and understand it to be true to who you are.

There was a new sheriff in town. We weren't taking the crap we took before, and we weren't laying down any longer. We were not lying down to our self anymore; we were going to become the master and no longer be mastered by self. As painful as it was, I definitely now know that I taught people how to treat me. So, the only person that I could be really upset with was me. When all the dust was settled, it was all too clear that people were content with being loyal to them, and they could care less about what was going on with your loyalty to self. Sounds to me like a bunch of codependency.

If I over thought it, a part of me was lowkey angry with some of the people I called friends or other amazing individuals that were around me. I felt I helped aid them in being great, and no one ever thought to ask me what I wanted to do with my life, what I wanted for my future, how they could assist me walking in my greatness. When I went from understanding to overstanding, I realized that it was nobody's responsibility but my own to make sure my greatness was not only nurtured but cultivated and lived out to its fullest.

Objective gaze

So, when I got out of my feelings, I could be realistic with myself by not projecting blame on others because of how I felt about myself. This reality changed everything; why did it take so long for this to click? Growing in knowledge of this created the version of myself I needed. I started creating boundaries, saying no when I meant no. I was my first line of defense, and it was up to me to stand up for myself now. Dare I give that responsibility to someone else? When I can now be intentional with myself. Giving myself to myself, being intentional with my words, thoughts, and deeds towards myself. I've learned to be selective in where I was investing my time and choosing who was allowed to deposit or make withdrawals.

Being intentional totally went against my motto at the time; the one I lived by. Good things come to those that wait. It seems that I was letting this statement use me instead of me using it. Clearly, I kept it as an excuse not to go my hardest or go above and beyond for myself. Good things come to those that wait, I believed. Until this one fine day where I read something that knocked the breath out of me. It said, "Anyone who says good things come to those that wait is probably STILL WAITING!" Ouch, I felt that in the deepest part of me. I had set myself up to be FOUND WAITING on something else besides myself to show up.

I had, without knowing, slowed myself down. I was looking for something else to come to save the day. I now know that I'm who I was waiting on. I am the key that will unlock the mystical and magical things about me that will lead me to my true destiny. Your divinity has arrived, and it's been waiting for you. We're in a position to wait no longer. I will not stand at the door, waiting for someone to open it. We have courage, a blood-bought right, and a really good reason this time.

"I'm that reason!" Sierra, to the rescue!

❤ *The Early Years: 6-9* ❤

One of the earliest memories I have of myself is being in a car's back seat, looking out the window. I don't remember much about what I was gazing at in that moment, yet my heart smiles at the thought of this little girl. I can feel her very essence. This is not about what I can see, but what I feel. That is what makes this my favorite memory of myself. There was a moment where she chimed in on conversations between the adults in the car; I believe it was Patti and Erika. They had asked a question pertaining to a sign we passed a few miles back. They were curious about what the sign said. I was on time with the answer that neither of them could remember.

This was a normal thing for me, remembering things that I was not even focused on. Like I remember hearing the phone ring while I was playing or watching tv, one of the two. I don't recall who the person was, but at some point, they were asked to recite back a phone number that was just given, but they couldn't remember the number, and I was able to recite it for them. No one paid attention to my ability to do these things. I was only reminded of my own forgotten/hidden talents until I had the memory of this little girl sitting in the back seat looking out the window.

More than likely, we were headed to Saint Pete to visit my grandmother or go by my grandfather's house, either to check on him or for a cookout that he was having under the big oak tree in the front yard of his brick house. This is the only place we traveled that seemed like it took forever. I lived in Tarpon Springs at the time, and I remember it was an upstairs duplex that had a clothesline in the back. The walls were painted brown, and I remember days and nights sitting in the living room watching either wrestling, *Bionic Man, Bionic Woman,* or a bunch of other shows on the floor model television.

I'm more than certain that I went to school, although I don't have any memories of school at this moment. I do remember playing outside with the neighbors. We had two parks which people would call the big park and the little park. They were both about the same distance away from my house, and the only difference was to get to the little park, you had to go down the hill.

I remember one afternoon on our way to play, we were all on bicycles, and this particular bicycle that I was on was an old school bicycle that had the flap on the back where you could hold a newspaper or books of some sort. I remember sitting on that part as we went down this big hill, and then my next memory is the bicycle all of a sudden coming to a stop and us falling over. I don't remember who the operator of the bicycle was, but I do remember feeling excruciating pain. The bicycle had come to a stop due to my feet being caught in the bicycle's spokes, which meant it could no longer go down the hill.

I currently have a scar that confirms this memory. The scar is on my ankle of the foot that actually looks like it turns a different way when I walk. I don't remember going to a hospital, and I don't remember what kind of aid took place from this injury. During that time, I do remember crying about it, and I do remember the pain.

There's a memory of one Christmas where we all got bicycles. We were all outside playing, and we went to Uncle Mike's house. It was only me that laid my bicycle down and didn't put it up on a kickstand. Uncle Mike came out of the house, or another resident came out of the house, and they ran over my bicycle. This made the pedal of my bicycle come off, and we never got it fixed. I remember still attempting to ride the bicycle with one missing pedal. It was the only thing that was wrong with it, yet it was never fixed.

I remember a baby being born, my little cousin Staff and the babysitter that we used to go to would pick him up and drop him off while my mom went to work. I remember having shoe fights in the room, playing hide and go seek, I spy, late-night games of Goldfish and Uno, which is still one of my favorites. I remember sitting on the toilet seat for my sister because she didn't like to go to the bathroom if the seat was cold when she had to go. So, I would go to the bathroom and sit for a few minutes just to warm the seat up for her.

I remember having to go somewhere one day, maybe we were going to school, I'm not exactly sure, but I do remember I was half asleep on the bed, and Mom had the lights on. She was ironing the clothes, and the iron fell on my leg and burned me on my outer right thigh. It healed over time, but I look back at it years later because it is a wound I could never forget. The scar resembled the actual thing that caused it. I remember freshly made eggnog during the holidays.

I remember curry chicken and all types of great smells coming from the kitchen because Dad was an amazing cook. I learned a valuable lesson that everything that smells good might not be what you want. Those smells led me to the kitchen one day as Dad had been in there cooking all morning. We sat at the table cause, of course, we probably begged for it, or it was lunchtime, but it was some form of soup. I remember as we ate the soup, I started, you know, moving the spoon around in my bowl.

I know that I was super young, but I've seen octopuses on television before, so when I looked down in my bowl, and I saw that suction thing that I had only seen on the leg of an octopus, I broke down. I no longer wanted it, and I had to learn my lesson about asking for stuff when I didn't know what it was. Granted, I had to sit at the table for a little while with threats of, "You better eat it." Somehow, I managed to get out of that.

You better believe that no one was coming in the kitchen trying to take any bites of that. I can see the three of us sitting at the table, and I could never finish eating my food. I was always the last one sitting at the table, so to save me from my slothfulness while eating, my sister and my brother would sneak into the kitchen pretending that they were looking in the refrigerator for something and would take bites of my food away with them. But, when we were at my grandmother's house, she didn't play! I had to sit at the table until all my food was done.

It wasn't that the food was nasty, I just was not hungry, nor did I have a big appetite. Like, we would go to McDonald's and get happy meals, and everybody would always bet on who was going to eat the rest of my food because they knew that I was not going to finish all of it. The weekends were when we went to the laundromat to do laundry. After we loaded the car back up and were headed out of the parking lot down a little dirt road alleyway, all packed in the station wagon like sardines. Clothes in the back, kids on the back seat, and I remember sitting by the door. As we drove down the alley, and Mom turned the corner, I fell out the door, and she continued driving down the street. I could hear everybody screaming, telling her to stop.

Luckily, I only had a few scrapes and bruises because we weren't going quite that fast, but it's definitely something that stayed with me. I often remind the little ones of this story when they're in the car with me to get them to not lean on the door. Just because it appears closed, it might not be.

We were upstairs in the boy's room, and I was jumping up and down on the bed. On the way down from a jump, I landed on someone's head, and obviously, my tongue was slightly sticking out, probably from laughing from all the excitement. As I hit the top of my head, I bit down on my tongue, and instantly, blood filled my mouth. I had bitten a piece of my tongue off. I remember crying, but I don't remember what happened after that or what kind of care was performed.

I also had this tooth that was giving me a hard time as it was growing out of my gums. It wasn't painful, even though it seemed like it had been pushing its way out for some time. I remember being taken to the dentist, and of course, they numbed me so they could remove the tooth. They gave me a little plastic container that looked like a tooth that they placed my tooth in. I remember carrying it around; it had a string on it, so I was able to wear it as a necklace. That was cool until I lost the tooth somewhere. So, I threw away the container

I sometimes remember my cousin that lived in Saint Pete and would come up for the weekend from time to time. Her name is Erika, and she was the oldest of the grandchildren. She would come up for the summer and would babysit us. She had a friend that lived at the bottom of the hill whose name was Tina. Tina used to play with our navels and suck her forearm in a particular place. She obviously had been doing this for a long time because she had a black, purple, and nasty looking mark on her arm.

When we were playing and had dresses on, she would ask us to go put on shorts. While she sat there with my cousin and talked or watch television, she would play with our navels. This obviously provided her with some form of comfort. Somehow, I knew that every time, but whenever she wanted to do it, we all allowed her to, except for my brother Tony because he didn't like it so much.

There was this one time the house was pitch black; I don't recall if it was just nighttime or if it was like early in the morning before the sun came up. It was the three of us whispering and tiptoeing, trying to get downstairs to the kitchen for something. We must have discussed this and come up with a plan for this meeting because something had to have been masterminded for us to be up simultaneously. As we came together and tiptoed down the stairs, I wanted to say I was the first in line, of course. They would always have me be first. As we got to the bottom of the stairs, we could look and see the window of the living room.

As I turned the corner and took my last foot off the step, I looked up at this window and saw that somebody was looking back at me. There was a crack in the curtain, but they were clearly trying to see what they could see. They had their hands cuffed around their eyes and pressed against the glass as you do when you're trying to have a clear sight of something. I know I surprised him just as much as he surprised me. There went being quiet because I screamed so loud and beelined back up the stairs. Of course, now my parents were waking up, and we were all frantic and crying. We woke Dad up and came downstairs to check out the scene. Needless to say, whatever we were trying to go to the kitchen and get, I don't think we never got it.

❤ *Random Memories Weekend Adventures* ❤

I started to notice that I was a different little girl, not in the sense of feeling out of place, but because the way I felt was with my heart, and I saw life from a heart perspective. My ability to do this would grow to feel like a curse instead of a blessing when I grew up and realized that not everyone has that ability. I can remember someone waking up and staying in the house long enough to watch Saturday morning cartoons. *Tom and Jerry, Recess, Rugrats, Animaniacs,* just to name a few.

The moment they were over, we were out the door to embark on some kind of adventure. We would catch bus number 23 to the mall and hop off at Gulfport Beach on the way back home. We would sometimes walk from one side of town to the other. The youth nowadays have no idea what it means to use your Tom and Jerry. We would freely be outside playing all day, but we knew we were supposed to make it home before the sun went down. We also knew to be home before the street lights came on, or there were consequences to pay.

I remember the summertime games of kickball. I used to love it when the word got out, and everyone from the neighborhood came over. I remember Michael and Windle, who were twins, lived three streets over. Then, there was Earl and Luke; they stayed across the field in the corner house. LaToya, who stayed up the hill. Valerie and Talonda, who stayed next door. No one liked to play with my cousin Tony because he would always kick the ball so far that everybody on his team would make it to home base.

So, I just made sure I was always on his team. Red Light Green Light, Hide and Go Seek, and Hopscotch, were a few more games we all had fun playing. I remember a time we were in the field playing baseball, and my memory doesn't serve me very well because I don't recall who was there, but I do remember being hit in the head with the bat as I pretended to be the umpire.

I remember going into the house, crying, holding my head as I went to the backroom and laid on the couch. I never told any adult, which I know wasn't the smartest thing to do. I could have suffered from a coma, or my brain could have been bleeding, or anything. The only damage I suffered was a lump on my head. It was clear that my guardian angel was definitely looking out for me. I woke up from that moment because I'm writing this book, but I don't remember much about the rest of that day.

I can also remember being able to give advice to adult figures in my life about things I had never experienced. I also remember giving advice to this little girl down the street concerning the guys in the neighborhood. Since my cousin was the oldest boy in the neighborhood, she felt she needed to share with me what was happening. She told me they would go down to her house in the morning when her mother had left for work on the weekends. She had older brothers also, so the boys would meet at her house.

I explained to her that she didn't have to do anything that she did not want to do. We were sitting on this old truck outside of Miss

Jackie's house. She stayed two doors down from my grandmother, and I can remember it like it was yesterday. Sitting on the humps that were in the back of a pickup truck. We sat there and just talked and talked all afternoon.

I remember one Saturday afternoon, I was sitting in the backroom and could hear the ruckus of boy's voices entering the house. The next thing I knew, I was being jumped by all the boys in the neighborhood. Because my cousin was the oldest boy in the neighborhood, they knew where to find me. I had no idea why this was happening or what the cause was behind their actions. Later, I came to find out that they were upset with me because the young lady I gave advice to had actually decided to stand up to them. They were not happy, even though she was happy to say, "Sierra told me I did not have to."

There were actually some weekends where my mom said she would come and get my sister and me and take us someplace. She had a boyfriend named Jerry, who had crazy long fingernails like my grandad and a tremendous amount of hair on his face. I had never seen such a thing before meeting him. I had never seen a guy with so much facial hair, and he walked with a limp. He told us his limp was caused by him jumping out of a building when he was younger. The fall shifted his whole hip bone. He drove semi-trucks for a living, so they would often be on the road.

For whatever reason, when they did not come when they said that they would, I remember being teased by my other little cousins. How is it that I couldn't understand how this wasn't my fault? Of all these things that happened to me as an adult, hell, I still don't get it. How do we make fun of something or somebody for something that they have absolutely no control over?

On a brighter note, I remember them taking us to the circus. I remember always going to IHOP and eating pancakes. I remember short road trips with them, and I always thought he was a good man. But there goes that wisdom again. With my mother and him having an addiction, he didn't have to bring this woman to see her kids. He didn't have to consider the fact that she was a mother, and later I would grow up to find out that those very thoughts that I had actually happened. Some children whose mothers were drug addicts put the men in their life before their children. I knew from my wisdom that my mom didn't have a job, so whenever we went and did anything, this man was definitely providing for us to do those things.

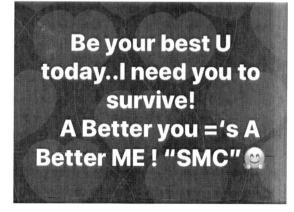

Be your best U today..I need you to survive! A Better you ='s A Better ME ! "SMC"

CHAPTER 2

∞ Identity Crisis ∞

It had to be the weekend or summer because we were at my grandma's house. When she had a snack for us, she would often call us into her room one by one and give us a treat. We had to eat in her room. I would either sit next to her on the bed or in the chair that sat in the corner. I had no idea that this snack time would be like no other. I was not focusing on my present moment, lost in the yummy thoughts of savoring every bit of my snack. I don't recall what kind of snack it was, but usually, it was some kind of Debbie cake or some little sweet thing.

My grandmother said to me—and I don't recall her exact words yet to this day—but I was told that my mother, the woman I've been calling mom, was not my biological mother, but my Aunt Patti, my biological mother's youngest sister and number three of the four girls my grandma had. I still don't remember saying anything back. She told me that Duke is my mother. A numbness came all over me, and it was crippling. I don't even remember leaving her room to this day. This news felt like a bomb; it snatched me out of my yummy state really quick.

So much time after that snack in my grandmother's room is a big blur. I have to think now that she informed the rest of the family that she had finally told me who my real mother is. Everything looked the same, yet I could feel the difference. Instantly, everything changed. I felt like a stranger amongst the people I once knew as my family. I went from having an ideal family (according to society) consisting of a dad, mom, brother, and sisters. Now, I was the child of the crack head of the family, and I don't know who my father is.

Instantly, I began to be picked on by my cousin and kids at school for something I didn't have any control over. How cruel is that for a little person to have to deal with? Because of the way others treated me due to my situation, I grew up thinking that it was something wrong with me. That lead to thoughts of not being good enough.

I was unaware of the effect that this would have on my life and my decisions as an adolescent and long into my adult life. In knowing what I know now and what I experienced, I spent all this time trying to convince myself that I am worth loving, and there is definitely something unique and out of this world about me. Yet the lies I had told myself had overshadowed that truth I felt about myself, so much so that I actually started believing them. I would come up with M.U.S (made up stories) to seem normal, especially while at school. When the other children would be talking about how their mommy and daddy did this or did that, I would often make up a story to convince them that I, too, had a mom and dad at home that was doing the same things.

I felt then like they were bragging and throwing it in my face like they knew my truth. I was now fatherless, and my mom was the one you heard the family talking about. I felt like they singled me out. They teased us like my mother was the only crackhead in the family, even my sister, and brother. Well, now my first cousins had no problem joining in on the crackhead jokes. I felt like an outsider as if that wasn't enough for a little girl to take.

Out of the group of first cousins came a sister. Pokey is her nickname, Shekina is her name. Come to find out, me and this girl had the same mother and father. From what I now understand, when they became concerned about the way my mother was caring for us, they decided to intervene. I went to stay with Auntie Patti, and Auntie Wanda was raising my sister. I'm sure that they did what they felt was best, but personally, I don't think our sisterly bond ever recovered from the separation. To this day, it still seems to be a struggle. I don't know what life was like for her before she was introduced to me as my sister because it seems we only have a connection when it's driven by pain.

connection only by emotional pain

∞ *Forever Changed* ∞

By the age of nine and a half, or ten, we were no longer taking those road trips to visit grandma on the weekend or for summer break. I mention that because we had been living there for a while, and it was at the age of eleven when the tragedy happened that I'm about to reveal to you. We moved from Tarpon Springs and were now living at my grandmother's house where Auntie Wanda and her daughter Erica, the same cousin who would come to Tarpon Springs during the summer, shared a room. In the room next to theirs was my two cousins, Talisha and Joe, who were brother and sister, also shared a room. These were my Auntie Chantay's only kids at the time.

In the room next to theirs was my grandmother's room. That same room where snack time had become my worst nightmare. Pokey and I slept on the floor in Auntie Wanda's room, and she would make a palette for us to sleep on.

I can remember the smells of her night time face routine. She did it every night after she'd finish rolling her hair with hair rollers. She would tie her scarf around her head before she would begin. Sitting straight up in the bed with her back against the headboard, she would pull out the mirror and place the handle part in between her thighs with the mirror facing her. At this moment, she seemed to take great pleasure as she started to unfold.

The aroma of green alcohol would tickle my nose and then the sweet smell of her Oil of Olay that she would put under her eyes. All the while, she would repeatedly tell us to close our eyes and go to sleep. The TV shows *Dear John, Cheers,* and *Three's Company* are some of the shows I can recall her watching. Oh yeah, then there was *Murder She Wrote, Perry Mason,* and *Knight Rider,* which is the one I'd end up falling asleep on. Pokey was always asleep before me.

We slept in between the two beds with my cousin Erica on my right and Auntie Wanda on my left. She would leave the closet light on with the door cracked so a hint of light could shine in the room, just in case we had to get up and go to the bathroom in the middle of the night. We didn't have a washer and a dryer. I guess going to the laundromat wasn't something we could always afford. I just remember having a bucket of clothes with some form of detergent in it, and we would wash our clothes on the front porch and hang them on the line in the backyard to dry. When we didn't speak up that we needed clothes washed, we would often have no socks or clean underwear, so you ended up washing them out the night before. We would hang our clothes on the fan to dry them and hope that they would dry.

I remember having those yellow stains on my socks and my white Keds if you didn't rinse the bleach completely out. Keds were a popular shoe back then. Also, from using too much bleach, you could smell like pee, so I was told. I remember a girl on the bus started picking on me because she said I smelled like pee. The bus was crowded that day, too; some people were sitting three to a seat. She was like, "Is that you that smells like pee?" I looked right at her and just told her no, but I knew what she was referring to.

Apparently, she could smell the strong aroma of bleach from the socks that I had washed out and half-dried that morning, so I could have a clean pair of socks to wear to school that day. So, she repeated herself, but louder this time so everyone on the bus could hear her,

"You smell like pee!"

I was so confused; I didn't understand why she would scream that announcement out so loud? Especially after she asked me, and I explained to her what the smell was. Again, hard for me to wrap my brain around people...I couldn't understand why people picked on you for things you had no control over. I just couldn't understand why we couldn't all get along.

I remember having to get your own switch off the tree to get a whooping, which, for me, didn't happen very often. It only took me one or two times before I realized I did not like it, so I always did what I was told to do.

My grandmother was not big on family fighting. I remember when we would bicker amongst each other, she would tell us that you're supposed to do right by family. I comprehended exactly what she meant by that so much that I took it very seriously when she said it. Even when it came to cracking jokes back or fighting, I would remember what she said, that we will always need family.

One time, I remember fighting my cousin Joe in my grandmother's front living room. I was getting the best of him, and my grandma screamed for us to stop. She screamed, "You don't fight family." So, I stopped fighting him, and he kicked me in my stomach; oh, the pain! I remember curling up like a big ole ball on the couch, crying.

I never cracked jokes back or picked fights like everybody else. I couldn't understand, even at this age, why you would want to say something to hurt someone intentionally. I remember those weekends, hanging out with my big cousin Erica, she was into music, and she had a record player. We used to create a whole vibe; the roll-out windows were opened, the curtains were pulled back, and we talked and listened to music.

I remember listening to the song *I'm Not Your Superwoman* by Karyn White. Erica also loved Michael Jackson; she had the glove and everything. LL Cool J in her mind was her baby daddy and future husband. There was also a Salt and Pepper and Fat Boys kind of vibe going on. I remember we got hungry one time; she made this sandwich I'll never forget. I believe that was my first time having a B.L.T; it was so good. Let me tell you the secret, add parmesan cheese. SHHHH, don't tell her I told you.

Erica had friends who would come over. Two of them were her guy friends, named Pokey and Doe Doe. I was drawn to Doe Doe; he was a real live giant. I liked him; he had this joy about him that I could feel. He felt like I felt on the inside. He resonated with a feeling that I knew lived on the inside of me. I knew it was there, I just didn't know how to tap into it.

When he came over, it was like I found that part of me, just on the outside. He always had nice things to say, and he was always smiling. It was like he never let anything bother him. It was almost like he had this forcefield built around him. If it wasn't anything good, it couldn't come in, and he stayed in that place, and he lived there.

Donna was also Erica's friend, who lived up the hill from us, who came over from time to time. I'm not 100% certain, but we can assume that they went to school together. They were older than me, so I don't remember, but it was clear how badly Donna wanted to be some kind of artist. She was into music and choreography kind of stuff. One time, she gathered some of the children from the neighborhood and created this dance routine to Janet Jackson's song, *Nasty*.

When the song had gotten to a certain part that said, "Who's that in that nasty car?" we were supposed to turn around. She had us standing along the side of the street to do this dance routine. The moment we turned around, a creepy guy named Mr. Butler was driving down the street at that exact time.

We just considered him creepy. We never really saw him unless he was getting in or out of the car. He would either be leaving or coming from somewhere. He had white, silver hair on his head and a mustache on his face, and I don't know why, but we deemed him scary and spooky. Yet, that didn't stop us from always being in his orange tree, even though he didn't like us in his tree.

One day, he came to the door and said, "Get out of my orange tree!" so that could be where we got the story of Mr. Butler being scary.

Almost everybody in my neighborhood had some form of fruit growing in their front or backyard. I know this because we would take our time going from house to house with our bags, taking what we could.

I remember being in the room off of the kitchen where I was doing something, and I heard a knock at the door. I went to answer it, and it was Ms. Willie B, my grandma's best friend who lived next door. She told me to tell my grandma she was ready to go to the store. I had just gotten back from school not too long ago as my grandmother left out the front door. She left instructions to stay in the house and said that my aunt would be home shortly, and just like grandma said, Auntie Wanda came home not too long after Grandma left.

I told my aunt that my grandma had just left to go to Food Lion (the local grocery store) with Ms. Willie B and went back to my room and played. Before I knew it, there was another knock on the door. Again, there stood Ms. Willie B. behind the metal mesh door. She asked for Auntie Wanda. I noticed my grandma wasn't outside with things for me to bring in because I always helped her bring things in after she went to the store, so I went about my day. As I walked back to my room, I heard Ms. Willie B. say that grandma passed out in the store.

I remember going back to my room, where I was inspired, convinced, or I had a desire. I'm not exactly sure how I could put it, but I went back to that room and wrote a poem. There was no hesitation or concentration about it as if the time had already known the moment that had met it. This definitely was the first time I allowed an ink pen to express how I was feeling; it was my first poem. The house started to fill with people, and they talked amongst themselves. I can't remember who broke the news because I was still numb from my identity being shattered, and now this. They agreed to pull the plug (whatever that meant) the next day, and it was clear that my grandma wasn't coming back from the store.

I was too young to know at that time, yet I now wish I had visited Ms. Willie B's house; she had lost her best friend. Now knowing the sting that death leaves, I wish I could have brought her some sort of comfort. I wish I could just be there to hold her hand. I don't know how long she and my grandmother had been friends, but I know it exceeded my life span. Ms. Willie B had her grandchildren living with her, who we often played with.

Valerie and Talonda were their names. Valerie was tall, taller than any girl I had seen our age. She was brown-skinned with long, black hair. Her sister Talonda was the opposite, as she had a Jerry curl with bright skin. They reminded me of Pokey and I because they, too, lived with their grandmother. Also, I was brown-skinned, and Pokey was light. Really, I don't know all the details of their story, but I know some parts were similar to mine and my sister's.

∞ *New Normal* ∞

I don't remember much of the emotional state I was in; I think I was still in shock. I remember the powder-light pink dress she laid in the casket in. I searched my memories for this information, but I couldn't admit or deny if I stood alongside the casket looking down at her. I was reminded of something I do remember. I remember it like it was yesterday. I was sitting outside on the sidewalk in front of Smith Funeral Home, sobbing.

Casual life at Grandma's was not the same; normal play was no longer that. My new sister and I were the big jokes of the family. Well, I'll say from my little cousins, who had no problem with joining in on the games of picking on us and taunting us because my mom is a crack head. My father wasn't around, so as you see, this painful life went on without Grandma. In spite of it all, I went on being that intriguing little girl, remembering things and giving out advice far past my years.

What felt like days later, perhaps weeks, my grandfather passed away. It was definitely too soon to be trying to process this left hook that my family just got hit with.

Also, to this day, I'm uncertain of the cause of death, but I do know he went to dialysis twice a week. He was born in Belize, made his way here, and married my grandmother. They had five kids, and he was a loving man who was definitely all about his family. He had silver, curly hair, even the hair that was coming out of his ears. He had extremely long fingernails and toenails. He wouldn't cut them, so he'd wear his shoes a size bigger rather than have them cut down.

He taught me how to drive somewhat. I have strong memories of me sitting on his lap and controlling the steering wheel, using my blinkers, and checking my blind spots before switching lanes. I even got to honk at people who weren't paying attention while they were driving as he worked the pedals. These were things that I remember.

He would always have family gatherings in the front yard under the oak tree. He loved his grandchildren and would buy all kinds of food for us. I remember all my little cousins would be there, and he sent us on trips to our local farm store to get him a bottle of soda water. That is what he called it. There was hardly a time that you wouldn't find him chewing on something, even if it was an actual stick that I saw him pick up off the ground. He would lightly dust the dirt off of it before beginning to chew on it. Or, it was a chicken bone or a bone of some sort. He had these eyes; they had this blue tent around them, and he always had a hat on his head.

These are some things that crossed my mind as I sat in the same spot in front of Smith Funeral Home, the place I never wish to be again, sobbing uncontrollably. The white doves, the folding of the American flag, and the stiff man wearing white gloves. These are some of the images I remember before they placed the casket in the ground. It wouldn't be until later, when watching a TV show, that I realized that all of these things were because my grandfather was a part of the military.

I remember hearing stories that they found money in Granddaddy's wooden floors. I remember the day after the funeral when we were over at my grandfather's house. I wasn't sure what everybody was doing, but I made my way into the downstairs apartment where he spent most of his time. I couldn't believe he wasn't sitting there when I came in the door.

This was now my second encounter with death in only what seemed a matter of days apart. I felt this pain of death that is still with me today; it is one that tomorrow cannot heal. I sat on the couch in the spot he used to sit in, right by the door. I walked through the apartment, taking deep breaths of the smells of him that still lingered in the air.

My soul and my heart reached out as I attempted to wrap my arms around him, to embrace the very essence of him. Grandad had this music box that was shaped like a church, and it played Amazing Grace. I remember taking it so I could have something to remember him by. I hid it because I didn't want anyone to take it from me.

Auntie Wanda and Erica moved to my grandfather's house. I think I was in the 6th grade at this time, going to Madeira beach middle school. My cousin Talisha, being two years older than me, was in eighth grade. She had a group of girls that she hung out with inside and outside of school. They even had some rivalry with another group of girls. I remember some of the stories, but even at school, they often were seen fighting in the hallways. They usually had locks and blades. They could get down; they used to kick butt!

Ironically, this was where my first fight was if you want to call it that. It was with this girl named Lori. I had stayed after school for a pep rally. Although I can see her face, I can't recall the girl's name who tried really hard to boost us up to fight. I remember us standing across from each other, just looking at each other with the same puzzled look. They really wanted us to fight for some reason. They were on some, "The baddest one hit my hand" stuff. At one point, they even took our hands and hit each other in the face at different times.

People gathered, and a crowd was circling around us as they do when a fight is about to happen. As we were still standing there looking at each other, this girl was still egging on this battle between Lori and I. Even with a crowd gathered around, it didn't convince us that we should be getting physical with each other

I also remember the house parties that we used to have and how I had to stay in a room because they said I was too young to actually attend the party. So, I sat in a room listening to the music; it was definitely some jam pony going on. The DJ was always doing his thing! Now ya'll know, it's the music that keeps the party jumping.

As the DJ played all the jams, he had me wishing I was out there. But, it never failed. My cousin Talisha's boyfriend always shut down the party. He'd always end up getting into it with someone. Everybody was exiting the house and beginning to go home, maybe we had a few stragglers, but mostly everyone was outside. Of course, the DJ still had the music playing even though everyone was outside trying to see what was going on with all the fighting.

This was the moment I had been waiting on, I could come out of the room. The music was still going, so I helped myself to the dance floor, and I would dance by myself. I have no problem with dancing by myself. I actually get great pleasure out of doing it too. I closed my eyes and rode the beat of the music to feel it in my core, down to my toes. I had a smile on my face as I rolled my hips and licked my lips, becoming one with the beat.

I have to admit that there was a time or two I got to dance with somebody on that dance floor. The parties were always at our house, so you rarely ever heard of any other house party in the neighborhood. I had my first kiss at one of those house parties; it was a night like I just described. My cousin's boyfriend had shut down the party, the floor was empty, and the music was still going. "Hey, Mr. DJ," was bumping through the speakers. Of course, I made my way to the dance floor. I was in my own world, riding a wave to the beat. I heard the front door close as it was a metal door.

Interrupting my wave, I made my way to see who it was and because I had a new appreciation for the dark, I could tell who it was. I would like to think they knew who I was too. Perhaps he liked the dark as I did? I didn't think this then, but as I write this, I want to say thank you, Grandmother, for taking the fear out of the dark!! Who would've thought of the ways it would come in handy? Elnora put me up on my game.

There are also memories of me curling my hair, trying to copy my cousin Talisha on some of her hairdos. I definitely was left with my ears and my forehead burnt. At some point, my cousin Talisha and Joe had gone to live with their grandmother, their fathers' mother.

∞ School,
The Golden Rule ∞

I learned early on from these tragic experiences that the people who should love you don't, and the ones that you love don't stay around. I didn't know it then, but I built myself a fortified place to hide away from anything that could love me or that I could love. A safe place that later I'd grow up to realize, that not only did I do a damn good job of keeping love out, but I did an even better job of keeping myself in.

I can do better by myself than my parents or the adults did. I don't remember much about my school days, especially elementary. I have one memory of my kindergarten teacher, who I don't even think was my teacher. She was known for being mean to all the kids.

Memory number two was of third grade. I believe it was picture day; I remember having on this yellow and white pleated skirt with a solid yellow shirt. Also, there was the disappointment of being retained in the third grade for not passing math.

I didn't do much homework, nor were there any adults inquiring about my homework. I never sat down at a table and went over my spelling words or studied for a spelling test. I remember thinking, I can't wait to grow up so I can do better by myself. I have four memories from fifth grade that stand out, one being a patrol, and the other was having my hair checked for hair lice three times.

Miss Campbell taught my reading class, I think? Hey, I said I didn't remember much like this other teacher's name or what subject he taught. I'll go with science. I remember him giving us a piece of candy that you could eat the paper as it dissolved in your mouth.

I had a friend named Danielle, we were in a class together, but I don't remember which one. She invited me to go camping with her family for one weekend. I'm sure I had to ask someone for permission, although I don't recall who. But, I had got all my things ready to go camping when I left for school that Friday morning. I carried my packed items with me, right along with my school books.

I got to experience what being a car rider was like because her parents picked us up from school that day. I had such a great time. I'm sure this was when I learned of my connection with nature. For my first time, I experienced the catching of fireflies, walking barefoot in the woods, and the crackling of the wood from the burning fire.

Setting up the tent for sleeping was pretty cool. I was going to sleep under the stars. I felt so at home out in nature under the stars. I never once wondered what was on television. I didn't even wonder what everybody was doing back at home. I wondered if they even remembered that I told them where I was going or that I would be gone for the weekend.

Yeah, my love for nature was definitely birthed from this time and space. It was time to take the tent down and pack things up to head home. I also grew fond of the darkness because I understood it in some kind of way. I was happy to feel this way about the darkness because I remember, at some point, having a complex with it. The house would get really dark when it rained, and my grandmother would flip the breaker box when she got mad at us. She would make sure all the lights went off.

I remember us having a conversation, not sure how it came up, but I remember telling her that I was afraid of the dark. She told me, "If I wasn't so bad, I wouldn't be afraid." I still scratch my head on this to this day, but whatever she meant by it, I understood it. I'm no longer afraid of the dark because I know I'm not a bad person. They dropped me off back home, and my life went back to normal.

I was excited to return to school on Monday to share and reminisce about the amazing weekend I had. When I got back to school, things were different. Danielle seemed to be avoiding me. As time went on, I realized that's exactly what she was doing because she never spoke to me again. I was a little confused by her actions because I considered her, I guess you can say, my best friend.

The look on the driver's face when we got picked up from the car circle that Friday afternoon before camping, along with a few whispers that I pretended not to hear over the weekend. I wondered when she asked if I could come camping, she mentioned that I was a black kid. My heart tells me it was out of her control.

Those are just about all the things that I remember about elementary school. Guess who was finally in middle school? Morgan Fitzgerald, to be exact. I knew I needed to go to school, but there wasn't much that made me want to go half the time. I never considered myself popular or even felt like I was important to many. At least, not outside of what I could do for them.

I didn't go to school, or I came late. We would catch the bus, then leave and go to the mall to steal something. We would then head to school to play around in the hallways and ride the bus back home in the afternoon. One day, the teacher assistant walked in and passed a note to Mr. Bush, my English teacher. He said, "Sierra, they are requesting you to come to the guidance office."

I was so excited about leaving class, I hopped up. I took my time reporting to the office; as I stopped by some classes, I stuck my head in a few doors. I said hi to my friends as I walked by and looked through classroom windows. I was making funny faces at people while they were trying to do their work. When I finally arrived at the guidance office, the lady pointed me to the backroom.

When I opened the door, I saw two adults and a handful of people. Some I knew by name, and others I knew in passing in the hallways. The chairs were in an open circle facing each other. Then, a gentleman introduced himself as Mr. Oliver and proceeded to say they were here to tell us about an in-school and after-school program called Beta.

It was a program put in place to assist black, low-income families with children. It would be a place where we could come and learn. Where we could get help with homework and be mentored. Now, I have been told by Mr. Oliver many times to this day that I spent most of my time looking at the carpet during these sessions, and my answer to everything was, "I don't know!"

I didn't like that part of me. I would say, "I don't know," even when I did know the answer to the question. I was very shy and timid, always afraid to speak up and to speak out. I know my body language displayed my excitement about having a safe place to go. A place where people that looked like you actually cared about you and wanted the best for you.

Beta definitely planted some seeds, seeds that I wasn't even aware of. Beta was the first thing that happened naturally. Something that I didn't play a part in placing in my life. At this point, no one cared about my future, but me, it seemed. And, I was a child, so there was only so much I could do to make sure my future was bright. It was here that I'd be shown things and taken to places I probably would have never traveled to if it wasn't for them.

Particularly Mr. O and Mrs. Bj. They made sure I went on every trip, even when I didn't have the money. It was here that I would be introduced to things I wouldn't be able to identify until some years and lessons later.

That spring break, Shiviah and I spent some time with Mrs. Bj, and she loved on us. We spent a lot of late nights staying up talking. We went shopping and got our hair done. We went with the short Toni Braxton look, no more microwave ponytails, at least for me anyway because, at this point, I was doing microwave ponytails for several different girls at several different schools. I never thought to charge them, as long as they brought the hair. It was definitely a cool spring break.

I was happy to be back at school! Yeah, I know you thought you would never hear me say that. My favorite teacher's name was Dana Gray, and I think she taught science. I love that I wrote that, or even thought of her as being my favorite teacher; you would think I would know what subject she taught. I said she was my favorite teacher, not that she taught my favorite subject; there's a difference.

I liked her because she could see through me. I was misbehaving and acting out, only because of the pain and hurt I was feeling on the inside. She knew there was more to me, despite what I was giving. She told me one day she expected more from me, and I couldn't identify with that. Her saying she expected more from me gave me the idea that there was something more I had to give. She could tell that I was pretending to be someone else.

I had an option for the first time. I could either be the person I was giving or tap into the more of me that I was covering up. She called me out on it. I didn't like it, but from that day, she became my favorite teacher. Also, she looked like me, except her melanin was a lot darker.

She was a beautiful woman that wore that popular mood lipstick. I think she had some military background or something because she was definitely strict; you could tell she was structured. She knew what she wanted, and she took teaching those who looked like her very seriously, which I didn't know then.

Morgan Middle School had an African American male as a principal. His name was Mr. Tampa. They also had an African American woman as the guidance counselor. Her name was Ms. White. I didn't know how important, and just how rare it was, the things they had to go through to get those positions. I also didn't realize then the statement it made for me when I was going to school.

This image of individuals that looked like my family and me in positions of power gave me confidence that I wasn't aware of at that time. Without having any clue of their backgrounds or what they had to endure to be in those positions, I knew the sacrifices were worth it.

For a little black girl who was raised in the environment in which I was raised, no one told me that I could be a principal or a guidance counselor. But, to show up at school every day and see the opposite of what I had seen in elementary school was empowering and just a good feeling.

To feel like someone could actually have my best interests in mind and not treat me unfairly because of how I looked or where I lived. That little visual reminder during my day while walking down the halls, being greeted by Mr. Tampa, or seeing Mrs. White always gave me an extra boost in my confidence and my intelligence.

Mrs. White was a black woman that I saw take time and invest in the young, black girls at my school. I recall her being there for my sister as a mentor and a friend. My sister wasn't the only lucky girl that she went out of her regular job duties to make sure they knew they had someone they could trust and confide in.

CHAPTER 3

♥ Tables Turn ♥

Now with both grandparents being deceased, I understood the feeling when people said that certain people hold a family together (the rocks). With them both being gone, so much changed. I was now living with Wanda and my sister in my grandfather's house.

My mom and Jerry lived downstairs, and Auntie Patty and her children were living at my grandmother's house on Union Street. I had a big room, and the place had hardwood floors and lots of windows. Since my mom was living downstairs from me, I saw her every day.

The ground still hadn't leveled itself out from when the bomb was dropped about her. I kept my distance because my fortified kingdom was still standing. I remember Auntie Wanda telling me to pick up a piece of paper off the floor that I had been walking over for weeks when going to and from the bathroom. Her command came with threats of throwing it away if I had it, which I didn't, and she did just as she said she would.

Sadly, the paper was the poem I had written the day my grandmother never returned home. Perhaps that's why I avoided retrieving it from the floor, something I always regretted. I was starting to get a better understanding of doing better by me as if I was an adult. I felt as if I knew I needed more structure and guidance as a little girl like me should have.

I met this girl at the after-school program, and either way, we were now inseparable. We hung out so much that people really believed us when we told them we were sisters. So, one day, I decided to run away. I don't remember even taking clothes with me; I just up and left for an afternoon of play and never returned. No one looked for me, and I don't think the police were called. Although I was only four streets down and a few blocks over, it was still shocking that it didn't raise any alarms.

I now see that this was my attempt to provide myself with what I thought a child needed for their upbringing to become the adult who would be a good part of society. I might have been too young to have said the word society, but that wisdom I told you about definitely let me know that our lives are not our own. What we do affects all those around us, whether directly or indirectly. So, who we grow up and become definitely affects the whole world.

Auntie Wanda worked in the cafeteria at a local elementary school. I remember her in the all-white uniform, her hair tightly rolled because she put her rollers in the night before she was supposed to work. Because she worked in the cafeteria, she had to leave early in the morning, which meant that my sister and I were left in the house to get ourselves ready and off for school.

I had this old box radio where you would have to turn a knob to find the radio station, and I would turn that on very loud every morning when I got up. I had it loud enough to hear it while I was in the bathroom, brushing my teeth and washing my face. Sometimes, my friend Precious, or other people in the neighborhood, would come over, and we would have fun while on our way to the bus stop.

I think we played a silent game of musical houses because each morning, it happened to be a different house that we all just met up at. I guess whoever got ready the earliest that morning and was out the door determined whose house it would be for that day and as other people saw that person, they followed.

I was just a kid, having someone in the neighborhood that you happen to play with from time to time. As I write this book, I realize that I built long-lasting friendships. Still to this day, I talk to 75% of my childhood friends. Many I now call family.

I was still participating in the Beta program, although it was actually only like a six to eight-week thing. I had found a place that I felt could actually help me become a more responsible person. So later in life, I could be someone that gives to the world and not just takes from it.

I definitely just kept showing up to the meetings, although the group that I had originally started with had stopped coming. I didn't mention it was only down the street, so it was within walking distance, and they never turned me away. They allowed me to come, and I don't think I still had much to say at this point, but I knew that it was something that I needed. So, I was drawn to it, and I went out of the way to make sure I got it.

I remember coming home from school, and I had a band-aid across my face. Momma Duke asked me what happened, I told her there was a fight on the bus, and I got scratched. I had to lie to her because

Finding Sierra

I asked her if I could get a nose ring a few days before, and she told me no. I didn't listen and went to get one anyway.

Shiva had one, so I wanted one too. She was my sister; I mean, we were dying our hair alike, that honey blond that was more like orange-red. They called us the Strawberry Short Cake Twins

Momma Duke definitely is what they called, not being wrapped tight. I was scared of her, and it became more of a hassle trying to hide my nose ring from her. I decided to just take it off, even though there was a slight fear for my life if she would have found out.

❤ *I'm Going to be the Adult* ❤

There you have it. I finally decided to be the adult I needed. I moved in with my new sister Shiva, one of the girls I met in Beta. They had moved to Grove St., so now she lived closer to me. She stayed with her grandmother and her grandmother's daughters. They were from New York, and they welcomed me in with open arms. Staying there came with a little more discipline than what I was used to. I know now that I craved structure and discipline, everything our youth nowadays complains about.

We went to different schools, so I started skipping more. Sometimes we would go to each other's schools and hang out all day. We would hop from bathroom to bathroom closest to that person's class. We didn't go to every period, and we also walked the hallways, dodging the hall monitors, trying not to get caught while everyone else was in class.

I went to 16th St Middle, and she was going to Saint Pete High School. I remember one day skipping went wrong. I caught the bus, but I didn't have enough money to get a transfer. I knew better, and I felt like I was being told that was what I get for not going to school. It was one of those times that my spirit was teaching me a lesson. Doing things that I knew I should not be doing.

So, instead of jumping on the bus with no transfer like a group of girls were deciding to do as soon as the bus came, I decided to walk all the way home. I didn't have the courage to jump on the bus, or I think that it was a good lesson that I needed to learn. That would definitely teach me not to skip school. Ok, so going to school on a regular basis didn't change, but a lot did. Well, it did internally for me.

I realize that even as a child, my focus was never on the physical. I've always been focused on my spiritual. I was trying to manipulate my physical, hoping it would change how I felt about life and myself. I was trying to make sure I had a positive representation of people, places, and things that would internally change things in me. I was always trying not to feel the way I felt on the inside. It's always been an inward, outward journey for me.

When Shiva's grandma went to sleep, we would often sneak out of the house. We would go on some kind of adventure or just walk to visit James and Clifford. We knew them from Beta. James was like my best friend, and Clifford was my boyfriend. Being from New York, Shiva made sure we had a blade or a knife or something with us when we walked the streets at nighttime. She was into older guys; she was mature for her age, plus with that Brooklyn attitude, many guys our age were intimidated by her.

One day, a few of us from the neighborhood decided to go to the beauty supply store. I'm not certain who was buying something, but someone had a bright idea to steal out of the store while we were in there. Nothing about this part of the game plan felt good to me. It felt like my grandmother was warning me. At some point, I was sure

I heard her voice. It was so real that I had to look up. I didn't like this uneasy feeling, so I left them and walked back home.

About 10 to 15 minutes later, a police car pulled up, and they were in the back seat of the car. Yep, sure enough, they got caught stealing out of the store. I'm glad I listened to that voice. I couldn't wait to grow up and be an adult, not so I could be "fast," as some of the older women say, but so I could make a responsible decision for myself without needing the consent of a parent or guardian.

♥ *Is It Greener On the Other Side?* ♥

I finally saw what I had been looking for, or so I thought. It was a lady who lived two doors down from us. She had two little girls, a car, and a home. I would see them come and go. She displayed what mothering should look like to me. I couldn't really put it into words or explain it. It was a feeling I got when I would often stare at their little family. I noticed they went to school every day.

They were always dressed nicely; we had told ourselves that this was the piece we were missing, and we wanted it. I still struggle with the idea, or some would say not being able to wrap your brain around certain things.

But, it was my heart that couldn't do the wrapping around this one thing. What I couldn't understand for the life of me was why the explanation of my mother being a crackhead made her unable to be a mother. I didn't get how her being on crack was greater than the responsibility of being my mother.

I'm still very uncertain about what took place, but I remember entering into this big blue house that I often stood on the outside of, wondering about the lovely things that I felt like I was missing that were taking place inside.

Before I walked over the threshold of the door, standing there with the little bitty clothes that I had in my possession, I remember the oldest daughter saying to me that she had dreams of killing her mother.

I couldn't understand that because my mother didn't do any of the things that I often stood watching with envy from the opposite side of the street. How could she want to kill her? I said to myself

I was in a totally different world. I considered myself being adopted. I was a big sister to two little sisters, so it was my time to lead. I took honor in this new profound position. I remember baking cakes, and I remember preparing dinner and helping my little sisters with homework. I remember running up and down the stairs. I remember the love that I was getting that I never thought I deserved, but I always felt I wanted.

I remember finally going to get my ID, the mean lady making me learn all of those digits and my Social Security number. I also remember a time or two being on punishment. There was another group of friends that I had on the back street, and there was a cut between the two houses. We would often travel through to pass things or meet up to see each other.

The brother of this friend's name was Maurice. He actually became the first person that I could sit and talk to about a lot of those bombs and tragic things that happened to me earlier in life. He was the first person that actually stopped and wanted to listen to me. I always found it strange how people would always come to you for advice and be eager for your response or reply yet never think to ask you if you are ok.

He was the first person I felt saw past my façade. He was the first person I felt could see all the pain deep in my eyes when we talked. He would come and sit on the porch, and we would talk late into the night.

I remember being on punishment for something, and I was told not to go out of the house. There were two rules: 1. nobody in 2. nobody out! That is the order that was set in motion when mom left to go to work or was hanging out with the girls. I remember one day she came home and asked me what I did that day. I told her I cleaned the bathroom and whatever else took place that afternoon.

I also ended up telling on myself. I said Tootie called and needed some milk, so I met her in the cut with a cup of milk. I was not supposed to leave the house, and therefore my punishment got extended. I had just told on my own self. She said, "Don't tell me you left the house when you weren't supposed to leave the house." But, that's how my heart was set up. Telling the truth, even if it got me in more trouble for it.

Here I was, a big sister now, I had responsibilities. I was learning what accountability was. I was receiving the things that I felt I was always missing. Somehow, I knew I needed some type of structure. We desired love, and it often confused me in my later days of how, or why, my heart was the way it was. It wasn't that love wasn't taught to me; love just wasn't an example that was necessarily present.

Love wasn't love if it wasn't felt, from my perspective. I didn't feel like my upbringing gave me the amount of love I needed. Feeling like that was why I was on the search for love. So, when she started hitting me, I didn't see it as a problem; it didn't come to me as an alarm. My adopted mom's love came in the form of my skin being black and blue some days. I had no problem with that. I was like, "At least she sees me." We identified the black and blue as she cared enough that she wanted me to know she loved me, so she hit me.

I had come from a place where nobody sat down with me to do homework. I don't remember studying for a spelling test or studying at all, for that matter. It felt as if I was really free to do what I wanted to do, but I'm thankful I didn't have a list of things. I was drinking and smoking weed by the sixth grade. There were trips to the store by the school to buy quarts of old English beer, also known as 8 Ball.

So, to be in a place where you have rules and are held accountable for your actions was a totally new life for me. As time went on, that lovely voice spoke up and said to me that this wasn't the form of love I want you to consider as love.

I wasn't supposed to consider this type of treatment as love. So, I started to look at her when she would administer my discipline, as if I could speak to her soul by staring in her eyes, trying to communicate with her telepathically. It would be way later in my adult life that I became aware that I was an empath (a person with the paranormal ability to apprehend another individual's mental or emotional state). This would explain why I could always pick up on people's emotions and know there was more going on behind the scenes of the actual act of emotions displayed.

I wanted to ask her, who did this to you? There was that wisdom and knowledge thing again. I just knew there was more behind why this was being done to me. It was telling me that she was only repeating what was done to her. I also learned that what I craved, as far as the structure and discipline, the two sisters who currently had that from birth did not want it. They felt like it was the worst thing.

She worked, and we went to school. Not sure what she did for a living, but I know she went to work every day, always smelling good, lips popping, hair curled. Expressing all of her pure feminism, which was the second time that I actually saw a woman cater to herself. It was Auntie Wanda's face ritual times ten. She would have glasses of wine sometimes after work. I saw being a woman in a different expression. It was a beautiful thing to watch, much like the sunrise. You can see them glow.

Unaware of the point behind it all, there was a lady and her husband, who lived across the street. Mr. and Mrs. Landers. Mrs. Landers would often be outside as I came and went on my travels. Not sure what drew me to her, but I would talk to her in passing. It was as if she knew exactly what to say, she could tell what I was feeling and the stress I was in. Or, maybe the darkness that I was in because every time I spoke to her, she had the answer to my problem or said something to encourage me.

I would tell her what was on my heart, and she would always listen. One day, she said to me, "Sierra, everyone doesn't have the heart that you have." I'd later grow up and understand exactly what she meant by those words. Not understanding them then at that moment, I could only smile. I knew I cared about people deeply; it was like I could feel what they were feeling.

So, I believe she was telling me that I loved in a way that other people didn't. Finally, the reality had set in that the way I feel about people, the way that my heart feels, is not how others feel. That was devastating, yet the weight of that concept would grow in me later.

She would always buy me little things because I was always getting her something. I appreciated her time and for her talking to me. I wonder if she had any idea how much she was actually helping, how much light she was shining into my dark places. She is definitely one of the few people throughout this journey that we consider "filling in the blank people." I was definitely gifted with a handful of people who filled in blanks. People who stood in the gap to help me get from there to here.

So, I remember her calling me over as she said she had something for me. I had something in the house I needed to do, so I told her I would be by later on in the afternoon, and she said ok. She just wanted to make sure that I came by because she wanted to give me something she had bought.

After I took care of what I needed to do, some minor chores, I went over. It was always a delight to see her. There was always a welcoming presence when I went over there. She said she had gone to the mall, mentioning how her favorite store was JC Penney's. My heart just smiled with so much joy.

It was nice being thought of. It was nice to know that as she went along her day, she thought about me. By this time, I had already given her a card or two. I'm reminded of being excited coming from the Folk Fair because I had a gift for her; it was my first gift to her. I just wanted to express to her how much I appreciated her for taking the time out to listen. That meant the world to me, especially when you are carrying it on your back.

Mrs. Landers also announced that she and her husband decided that they were going to love on me. I was going to be their goddaughter, and I could call them (Mom & Dad) my godparents. They had two children, a boy, and a girl. Christopher and Erica, who was the oldest. This was great, I was excited, and my family was expanding. I always wanted a big sister.

From that day, I became a part of the family. She kept me fresh and fly with the latest Bongo outfits. More than anything, I was thankful for this new life with these amazing people. Life was starting to feel like what I had always thought my life should be like. This new life was coming with people who actually saw me and wanted to love on me. And guess what? This time it felt like love. It felt like what I had been searching for.

So much happened that I thought this was the piece to my missing puzzle. That blue house felt blue most days. I know it served a purpose, which is why I found myself loving her there still to this day. I harbor no ill feelings towards this lady. She was invited to my wedding. Her daughters are still my sisters, and she was also at my coming out 40th birthday party.

I lost my virginity in that blue house, not because I wanted to. Losing your virginity should be a sacred, important, memorable time for a girl, with someone you so-called love. I knew all that, but for some reason, I didn't wait for that. Even in thinking about it to write about it, I'm not sure what changed this particular day that I had the bright idea to no longer be a virgin anymore.

So, I took it upon myself to call all my friends. At that current moment, I was the only virgin left out of my clique. I decided to call to ask each and every one of them about their sexual experience. I make it sound like I called everyone in my phone book, but I only called three of my friends.

After I interviewed all of them, my mind was made up. I was going to lose my virginity. So, I planned for it and knew who the guy was going to be. It was someone I was currently dating, an upperclassman. That might be why I felt like I needed to lose my virginity because I knew I was dating an older guy, and he was not a virgin. Nevertheless, I shaved my legs and shaved other places too.

I made sure I had a candle lit, the music going, and I smelled good. It was over before I knew it. It was absolutely a lot faster and nothing like the way that was described to me when I interviewed my homegirls.

I was sadly disappointed, but with myself mostly. And do you know, this jive turkey went around telling people because it's a popular thing to sleep with a virgin. At this point, I had had it with some of the guys bringing this up because he was bragging about it. So finally, I told a bunch of his homeboys the truth. That he was a quick pumper, and I felt more pressure putting in a tampon.

Now when he hears my side of that story, I bet he won't brag about it so much. The weekend of my 16th birthday, we as a family said goodbye to that "blue" house, and we moved. Mom was dating this guy named Darrell that had two daughters, so now I had four sisters. I don't know what went on behind the scenes. I just knew that we were moving.

❤ Years 17–21
Running Away Again ❤

Disconnection

As a result of the move, my school zone changed. So, I had to go to North East High School in the second semester of my 10th-grade year. Even as I am writing this, things are connecting. I was definitely starting to see more of what I now identify as a dead man walking. Blank, blurry spaces in my life. Disconnecting was a survival tactic I had learned; I do it without even realizing it.

I said all that to say I don't remember much about my experience at this school besides a few details that pop in my head. Sadly, I don't recall any of my teacher's names, not even the teacher that I told about the abuse back home. Ok, yes, it was randomly said. I know he wasn't expecting it, which explains the reaction on his face that said he heard me but was acting as if he didn't hear anything.

I was in this class with two boys, Dontrelle and Darnell. You've heard the saying of the classroom clowns, but these two were the school clowns. They were just this amazing duo that kept you laughing on some unexpected outrageous entertainment. Needless to say, it was hard to ever get any work done.

I don't remember a whole lot about Northeast. I remember moments of standing in the breakfast line. I do know that I remember writing to my sister Pokey. We had not lost connection since I found out she was my sister. She was in some kind of program for her behavior. It was like this level program where she got knocked down a level if she did something she wasn't supposed to. We were each writing to each other often; I was trying to keep her encouraged and out of trouble so she could go to the next level.

I remember one day we skipped school, Tootie and I, and we were doing whatever. Actually, I don't think we skipped this day; I think we just left early. But, we found ourselves at the McDonald's on 4th Street, where my mom was working. I can't remember if that was a conscious decision or we just stumbled across that idea, but I remember my mom was upset. The manager would not allow her to have a break at that moment so she could come from behind the counter to talk to us, so we waited.

Finally, I remember standing in front of her, not remembering exactly what we were talking about when my friend Tootie told me to take off my sweater so she could see the black and blue marks. I wasn't sure what made her want to do that, but I denied everything. My mom was like, "Is that lady beating on you?"

I told her no, and I did not take off my sweater, but there went that wisdom again. That was far beyond my understanding because I knew if I had told my mother this, what good could have actually come of it? What was she going to do? Go to the lady's house and beat her up?

That would land her back in jail, where she just came from, or ruining my living situation. She didn't have a better place or space to provide for me. Also, what gives her the right to think that she had the right to beat up anybody? She wouldn't have to be a fill-in mother if she had decided to take on her role of being my mother. So, I lied, and we denied it. I think we sat down and ate McDonald's. We then moseyed on home later on that afternoon at the same time as if we had just gotten off the bus.

Different place, but nothing changed. I did all my chores, and I probably prepared dinner, which always came with a dessert. I always had to bake a cake of some sort, but once she came home, she was aware that I had left school due to the school calling her. How else could she have known if the school didn't call her? And of course, you know it was solved with more discipline. I never allowed her to see me cry. I always looked at her with looks of who did this to you? And, what did I do to deserve this?

A part of me was like, I should have just told my mother the truth when Tootie tried to get me to take my sweater off. But, that wisdom was far beyond my years. I knew that nothing good for me could come from that. My mom would've gotten mad wanting to fight, which could've sent her back to jail. She was already on probation, and looking at the bigger picture, she didn't have a better place for me to live. As I said, nothing good could have come from it. It would have made things completely worse.

I still hung around people from Osceola, although I was going to Northeast. I saw Precious, Crystal, and The Uglies, which had grown by the way, and a few other people that I went to Osceola with. Crystal and I now lived closer, so we started hanging out a lot more. Plus, Mr. Darrell was friends with her uncle, so we definitely spent a lot of time together. I always admired her. She had this confidence that stood out and stood tall. She had this amazing smile, also the giddiness of a 3-year-old little girl.

If all that wasn't unique enough about her, she also only had four toes on her right foot, but she had no shame in it. Rather, it just magnified her confidence. It was my birthday month, but it was hard to get excited, which was not normal. I had been dealing with a lot inwardly that was messing with me. I was feeling off-balance, just not in tune.

Still figuring myself out was a lot. I didn't know then that my internal GPS was saying, well more so screaming…rerouting. But, things felt strange. We'll use that for lack of understanding. Back then, it was like I was being led to do stuff I couldn't really explain. Like something told me to pack all my clothes up. I remember that dream, the dream I was warned about. I had it! I had that same dream where that sweet little voice told me about killing her mother.

I had kicked my habit of eating cornstarch, but with all this going on, I wanted to escape again. Since cornstarch had no taste, it was almost as if it became whatever I wanted to eat for comfort food. I had figured out that I was addicted to the stuff, which is why I kicked the habit. As I walked to the store to buy a box of cornstarch, I thought to myself the whole way. I had to be deeply wrapped up not to notice or hear all of the chaos going on.

It was a long afternoon, and my attention wouldn't let me focus. I could see a crowd of people and lots of police. It didn't look safe to continue on, so I turned around and walked back home. I celebrated the small victory because that gave me the willpower not to pick up a box of cornstarch.

I got home and turned on the news, and all the news channels were broadcasting about this guy named Tyrone Lewis. He was gunned down at the corner of 18th Ave and 16th Street South. This was the year Saint Pete got put on the map for rioting and protesting. To this day, history has repeated itself over and over again. Our African males are still senselessly gunned down. Not much change has come in that area, or we wouldn't need campaigns that say, "Not My Son." Let me not work myself up, that's a whole other book.

I had thoughts of leaving before, but I stayed to protect my little sister because she had turned her anger from them towards me. I was my sister's keeper, but after that, I realized I could no longer stay for the sake of them. That my life would be in danger if I stayed.

It was now a week before my 18th birthday. Mom was across the street at a house party one of the neighbors was throwing. I don't know how I knew, but I knew this was my window of opportunity. If I was ever going to go, it would have to be now. It all happened so fast. I'm sure I was in a state of intense anxiety.

I called my godmother and asked if she would come, and I didn't go into full detail. I sat down and talked to my little sisters, as I always did. I needed them to understand that I was trying to protect them from having issues like I did. I wanted them to know that I wasn't abandoning them, and I would always love them. The car pulled up, I got in, and she drove off.

CHAPTER 4

∞ I Am Not Your Mother ∞

I moved in with my mom and Jerry. They had a two-bedroom apartment, which meant I got my own room. It came furnished, which was cool because this time, I brought my clothes with me. It had a big bed that took up most of the room. Her smoking crack had not changed yet, she definitely never did it in front of me, but I knew what it smelled like by now. I remember one of those mobile hanger things that usually spelled out your name. I had made it in shop class with paper mâché, and it hung over my bed from the ceiling fan.

After school, I would go to my friend Precious' house, where I sometimes wouldn't come home from, not even on the weekends. Duke would know where to find me. I would call her, or she would call me to check-in. I remember there was a time where every day when we talked, I would say, "Mom, what are your plans for today?"

She would say, "Same as every day Pinky, trying to take over the world."

Weekends turned into every day, and I found myself with a bed and a place to put my clothes again. I realized now that there was a form of structure that I felt I lacked and desired. Some weekends consisted of going to Precious's older sister's house, Andrea, who I called Ms. Land. We would listen to old school jams, talk, reminisce, and cry sometimes.

She brought a sense of peace to my world. She was and still is a phenomenal mother. Currently, she is a mother of three. I called her Ms. Land, but as the years went by, she grew into being so much more in my life. A mother, a friend, a father, a leaning post, and my faith when I was weary. We were never usually down at the same time, so we were able to be these things for each other.

I'm not exactly sure how I did it, but I managed to go back to Osceola High School for my 11th-grade year. Precious attended Osceola, so this time, the friend I lived with was at the same school. There was no more skipping. I was going to school every day and living with what I felt like was the family I had always desired. I was finally on a normal routine, and I was still in connection with Mr. Oliver, whom I met from Beta.

I remember they were going on a trip to Orlando or somewhere, and I remember asking Precious's mother if it was ok if I went, and she said go ask your mother.

Puzzled at her reply, I said, "But you feed me, you love me, you provide a roof over my head. This is home for me."

She replied, "But I am not your mother."

Even more puzzled by her reply, my heart smiled even bigger. She was the first person who openly acknowledged my mother as being my mother, without connecting the fact that she used crack. She was the first person who respected her position and not her condition. Finally, someone who felt like I felt. The opportunity was now available because there was always someone who made it feel that it was not ok for me to love my mother as a mother because of her doing drugs. I will always appreciate and respect her for opening that door, for indirectly giving me the right to love my mother for her position, not her condition

∞ *Life, No Cap* ∞

I did not mention that I had to attend summer school and night school every year since the 10th grade to get enough credits to graduate. I remember hearing the statement, "Your teachers have their education. You have to get yours." It was not my first time having this statement thrown at me, but this time I guess it made so much more sense that I tried to do something to change that.

None of the grandchildren at this point had graduated. Awesome, I would be the first of my grandparent's grandchildren to walk across the stage. I would bring honor to my family. I never thought of it like that until now. My birthday was late, considering the statistics back then. I didn't turn five until after the actual school year had started. This meant I had to wait until the following year to start kindergarten, right before I turned six. Plus, with the addition of staying back in the third grade, I graduated at 19.

I was happy to be back at Osceola as I didn't like it at Northeast. I'm not sure what it was about it, I thought a little bit about it so I could try to explain, but nothing pops up. Having to be at Northeast would have stopped me from seeing my friends, and I would've hated it, not just disliked it.

I went back to Osceola the first day of my junior year as if I never even left. I am still surprised how the mean lady was able to register me in school because I don't ever remember going to my family asking for any personal information. I don't remember her even meeting any of them before graduation. No, maybe she saw my mom once or twice.

Those last two years in high school were somewhat entertaining. I guess it's safe to say that I was present for more moments. I'm not sure what changed, but to actually be able to say that feels good. I actually remember more moments with much less blurriness. I was part of a group that we called the "Uglies." I was known as Momma Ugly, and I was the only girl in this group at this point. I also remember being nominated for homecoming court.

I remember that same year, it was on my birthday, so it was definitely turn-up time. I also remember the tears that I cried. I remember even in those moments of what started to feel like a normal childhood, there were still signs that there was nothing normal about my life. My first job was when I was 15. I remember working to buy clothes, working to pay for grad night, paying for my senior pictures, and I can remember having to catch a ride to the homecoming game that I had to attend since I was nominated for homecoming court.

I was supposed to ride around the football field on the hood of a burgundy Corvette. It just so happened that my dress was burgundy also. I remember going to the hairdresser early that morning to get my hair done; I had to find a way there. When I finally got there, I saw the vibe of the atmosphere. You could see mothers and families gathered together to support the other kids in the homecoming court.

I remember the gentleman who was the star football player that walked me across the field. I remember witnessing the puzzled surprise on the gentleman's face when all I did was cry as he drove me around the football field. The cars that went before me, you could hear their family screaming their names from the bleachers. When it was my turn to circle past the bleachers, there was complete silence, yet it was so loud. It was muffled out by my sniffles and the screaming of my heart.

It was July 6th, 1999, graduation day!!! I had on a blue and white dress, white stockings, and white heels under my gown. I don't remember much of the actual walk across the stage to receive my diploma. Actually, it was only a certificate of completion, but I hadn't told anyone that at the moment, I was going to night school and summer school. I had not gotten all the credits I needed to graduate, but it was enough credits that I could receive a certificate of completion stating that I completed my four years of high school.

So, you see, everyone was excited except for me. I hadn't felt like anything was accomplished until I looked around me. It was a little different, I must say. My mother came out, my sister was there, and a few family members showed up. I actually had all three of my mothers there. This was a phenomenon in itself. I cried about not having one mother, now look, I had three, and they were all here to show their support for my graduation time.

Auntie Patty was there, Duke was there, and the mean lady who took me in was there. Now I call her a mean lady, not because of what I endured while living with her, but because I know she was angry. Not with me, but angry about something that clearly had happened to her, and she was just repeating the cycle with me.

Orange and blue were our school colors. I'm not sure where the idea came from, but a few of us had agreed to wear orange and blue for the last few days of school. Ricky, a guy from my school, was nominated for this task. He also lived in the neighborhood not too far from Ray Jax, the neighborhood meat market. He made his own starch from scratch, so he was responsible for putting the crease in my orange shorts. I mean, these shorts could stand up all by themselves; that's how much starch was on them.

∞ *O.H.S Flashbacks* ∞

I have fond memories of me and Marcus (Bread) running down the hallways, about to be late for class just about every day. One of my favorite pictures of us is us standing outside of this classroom in front of the orange lockers. I have this perplexed look on my face because I knew we had less than 30 seconds before the bell rang, and then we would late again. He had this big smile on his face. His voice was deep like the guy from *Boys to Men*. He went to night school with me. Mr. David (his dad), whose voice was deeper than his, would take us and pick us up. We would ride in the back of the truck, where I would enjoy the refreshing feel of the air rushing across my face. Plus, there was a smile on my face because I was chilling with my brother.

I remember leaving school with the Twins, we had a few sets of twins in school, but I'm sure everybody from the "O" knows which ones I'm talking about. We would leave from time to time, going to somebody's house to get high. My first time hitting a bong was on one of those adventures.

Dre Buck was a good judge of character; he drove a black regal or something. The important word in that sentence is drove. He would pick us up from school and take us to school; he was a cool kid.

There was this kid named Steven, he was tall and had black hair. It's said that he's into goths, but I didn't know much about that. I knew he liked to wear black everything. When I would be coming up the hallway, I sometimes remember they would be making fun of him. I stood up for him every time I saw it. I just didn't think it was fair that they were picking on him. He chose to wear black mostly, so what?

I remember saying to them, "He's not picking on you for wearing FUBU, he's not picking on you for liking Jordan's, so leave him alone! He likes to wear black; you decide to wear that, and he chose what he wanted to wear." I just couldn't understand it because nothing about what Steven chose to wear affected them. They were simply bullying him. My heart didn't like it. I didn't think it was fair that you pick on someone because they look different from you.

I don't miss getting up so early to catch the bus to the Northside. From one county to the other county. I guess it was to keep a balance in the numbers of blacks and whites in the school. There was nothing pleasant about being at the bus stop by 5:45 in the morning, especially when it was cold out. I remember Precious would keep the blow dryer hooked up so, in the morning, she would turn it on. When she went to brush her teeth and wash her face, she would get half-dressed and jump back in the bed and turn the blow dryer on under the covers.

By this time, Precious was no longer riding the regular school bus. She had a bus that came to the front door that would pick her and Trayvon up. We had to get him ready to be out the door also. Auntie Tam was right there every morning, making sure we didn't miss a beat.

I believe it was Memorial Day weekend or something; I know we didn't have to go to school that Monday. Cause it was a holiday, Latrece's family had a party, and I remember us sneaking some kind of alcohol. I had possession of the stolen goods. I put it in this plastic sports bottle and then put that in the freezer. I had this bright idea to grab it on the way to school that Tuesday morning.

I didn't know that alcohol did not freeze, but it was good and cold. We sat there, drinking our life away on the bus ride to school. We named did Fahla-la it was so good. I was definitely drunk. That was my first experience with alcohol to that extent. Cause although I used to drink, it was usually just beer.

Dre Buck, the wonderful Andre Buck, ended up taking me home early that day. I don't recall if I just showed up at home or if I called to let Auntie know I was on my way. I had a tooth pulled, and I was supposed to be taking the antibiotics. I let her believe that I didn't feel good because I had taken it without eating any food. When Precious and Trayvon got home from school, she told me she knew I left school because I was drinking. I think I was still in bed with my head under the covers. We never did that again.

I recall a time I needed to go to the restroom, and I didn't walk out like I usually do. Instead, I asked if I could have a hall pass to go to the bathroom. I was proud of myself because I hadn't stopped to goof off by knocking on classroom doors or stick my head in classrooms saying hi to my friends. I was giving myself a pat on the back. When I was on my way back from the bathroom, there was this boy. He was an upper-classman and one of the star football players. I used to see him in the cafeteria from time to time, but I changed my route so I didn't have to run into him. Something about him always made me uncomfortable. He would make gestures and try to get my attention, but I would ignore him.

Now, we were standing face to face in the hallway, he was at one end, and I was at the other end. But, I could tell he instantly knew who I was. I turned around and started to walk back in the opposite direction, trying not to make him aware that I did not want to walk in his direction. I heard the sound of the wind change, and it felt like fire was breathing down my back.

He started running after me. With the feeling of being prey, I started running too. I ran down the stairs back by Mr. Ziglar's class, but he caught up with me, grabbed me, and dragged me under the staircase.

I fought with him like my life depended on it. He was on top of me, putting all his weight on me; it was getting very hard to breathe. I was swinging my arms and kicking my legs. So much so that he gave up trying to pull down my pants and started trying to kiss me.

I never thought to scream, and I had almost given up. I had nothing more to give, no more fight left in me (I graduated at 96 pounds, and this guy had to be every bit of 150-175 pounds). I had no more strength to fight with.

Right before I almost tapped out, he finally gave up with what looked like a face of disappointment as he got up and walked away. I was too shaken up from that ordeal that I never made it back to class.

CHAPTER 5

❤ Adult Life ❤

L ife after high school became real adult, real fast. I'm sure the fact that I was hanging around an older group of girls at this time played a part in the innocence of life being taken away. There was definitely another world out there that I had no idea about. They were into things that I had never done or even thought about. I was always able to learn from other people's choices, especially their mistakes. It kind of gave me a cheat code to this thing called life. You don't always have to fall to learn something; you don't always have to suffer to reign.

awareness

I had a saying, "Things can't stay the same if you work hard and you pray." Finally, my hard work was paying off. I got my first apartment down the sidewalk from the alley I grew up in. I grew up snotty-nosed and barefoot in these streets; I knew this neighborhood like the back of my hand.

Auntie Wanda and Auntie Chantay, my mom's oldest and youngest sister, were now staying in the duplexes at the corner. It was family-owned property, part of my grandfather's Hugh Burgess Estate.

The apartment was a nice little one-bedroom, perfect for just me. But, as you know, I did nothing for just me. Since I was the first one out of my group to get an apartment after high school, my house was the house that everybody came to gather at. I remember nights coming home from doing a double, and it never failed. There was either a party going on or a party had just ended.

There were times I'd be stepping oversleeping and drunk bodies stretched across the floor as I made my way to my bedroom. It looked like a few randoms, but the majority of the faces came from my Ugly Crew.

One of the members was Iceberg, but he was never amongst the partiers and drunk bodies I came home to on numerous occasions. This was an individual that lived up to his name, cool, calm and collected. He would pop up periodically, and we formulated a bond together. Our time spent together would include us eating our favorite snacks, which were peanut butter and jelly sandwiches, over long talks, and sometimes tears. Iceberg was always someone I could see my reflection in because he would share the pain he held in that no one else in the Ugly Crew knew of. Through these talks and the time we spent together, I realized that you never know what a person is going through unless they share it with you.

I remember shortly after our last time seeing one another, The Ugly Crew was gathering to throw a surprise party for him. We all wondered where he was cause hours had passed, and no one had seen or heard from him. So, at first, it wasn't anything to sweat because he was always the last one to show up or was always hard to locate. He was always off on his own mission to be great.

The details are still unclear on how or why, but we received news of the tragic event that Iceberg was no longer with us. It shook the entire crew and made us all look at our lives differently. Here we were, thinking that we were all close enough to see one another's pain or lack of happiness.

I myself took it hard cause I lost someone who confided in me, which enabled me to see all the shit I was holding onto that no one else knew. We had an unspoken connection, my pain was unspoken, but his voice was mine through his openness and trust in me. See, everyone always came to me to release their weight and pain on me, but no one spoke my language of pain and disconnection like Iceberg did. Without this friend, brother, kindred spirit, I started to feel cold on the inside. I had a realization that my world really was filled with trash cans (people), and they were using me as the dump.

This loss actually opened my eyes and mind to the truth of those around me. I was able to not only view things differently but felt them differently also. The Ugly Crew continued on after this loss, but we were never the same after this, particularly me. I knew from then on that nothing about my world was benefitting me, and I was just a means to an end for people. I could no longer accept that, and I realized that it could have been me instead of Iceberg. I, too, had days where I thought about ending my life. Glad I didn't because had I done that, my story would only reflect how I was there for everyone else.

Now that nothing about my world was no longer the same, it led me down roads that were unfamiliar to me. As I journeyed down these uncharted territories, I became the trash that was dumped on me by people all these years. These habits that were forming were unnatural to me, and it went against everything that my internal self was comfortable with, believed in, and stood for.

For instance, this one particular trash bag that was dumped on me by the older girls I had befriended was beginning to display as part of my character. The choices I was making stemmed from this bag of tricks that I thought would solve my problems, but only left me further disconnected from my authentic self. The lesson I got from that was, I can't fix my problems with someone else's tools.

Time felt different. It was moving rapidly, it was like being sucked into a whirlwind, but instead of it being filled with trees, boats, houses, and barbecue grills, it was full of my emotions.

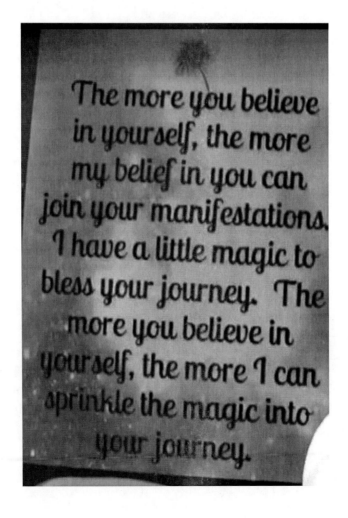

The more you believe in yourself, the more my belief in you can join your manifestations. I have a little magic to bless your journey. The more you believe in yourself, the more I can sprinkle the magic into your journey.

♥ *Shifting* ♥

Everything felt like it was coming undone. I had lost my apartment and just let go of my CNA job. The truth of the matter was, I was automatically terminated because I did a no call no show. I never told anyone. Never showing any signs of distress, but I was freaking out internally. That meant I didn't have money to pay rent. Everybody had eventually got the idea that we needed to abandon ship. I don't recall what announcement was made to update everyone on our code red situation.

I never told anyone about needing money for rent, nor was any offered. I cleaned out everything I was going to take out of the apartment and did a no call no show with the landlord too.

My forever friends were becoming just friends, not to the point of bad blood, hate, or anything. Life was just happening, and it was time to part and go our separate ways. This was devastating for me. I didn't ever think that this love would leave me too. Sometimes, you have to love people enough to let them go. I hadn't planned for a life without them. This definitely had to be another lesson I was supposed to learn. It hurt too bad to be anything else.

All of a sudden, a sermon I heard preached was brought to my recollection. It said, "Everyone won't be able to go where you're going," if my memory serves me correctly. It was talking about Joseph's story, and where he had to go, his brothers couldn't go with him.

This path could only be activated by way of his brother's selling him. They definitely did it with jealous intent. Turns out, it was the very thing he needed to get him on the path that echoed his name. Destiny had a plan and was calling him. I felt like I was being told not to take what happens to you so personally. It's neither good nor bad, nothing more, nothing less. It simply is what it is.

People are big on the "It is what it is" expression. Yet life has also taught me that it is what it isn't also.

It's the weight of a feeling, about a thought that creates the picture.

The picture you internalize will be the world you envision. In your words, thoughts, habits, and deeds, you live out and manifest it.

What I did keep of my things, I took up the street to Auntie Wanda's house. I would stay the night with my sister on the nights I was not at a friend's house, which was torture as I hate depending on people. Very few times do you get back what you put out. Now, to be in a place where I needed people wasn't easy for me. How easily do they forget when they needed my help? Of course, I had no problem helping them.

I now knew what it meant to watch TV until the television goes off. I believe I heard that from the lyrics of a song, it takes a fool to learn that love don't love nobody.

❤ *No, Not You* ❤

There were times life felt like it was screaming at me, trying to get my attention to tell me something. I had yet to understand what all that meant. Honestly, I am just now learning the importance of listening to it, that small still voice. It sounds like your own voice that speaks to you in a way only you know. I'll be upfront, I didn't always listen, which leads me down this path of memory lane where I realized that I couldn't do what everybody else did.

I remember having the signature "misunderstood" on my phone, and this lady who I knew loved me, and I greatly admired, told me that it was me who misunderstood myself. Life would scream, and I would ignore it, which always lead to a valuable lesson in the end. I was taught several different lessons that I couldn't do what everybody else did.

It was a weekend, so we wanted to go hang out. We decided to go to the club. It was jammed packed. The vibe was on point, and I was feeling good and minding my business. The music was bumping. I had my drink in my hand. Then, I heard a voice say, "You're not supposed to be in here. You shouldn't be in here."

Before I could formulate a rebuttal and go into defense mode, it spoke up again, saying, "I'm not talking about everyone else. I'm talking about you." So, I don't forget, there was a lesson attached to this message. Ironically, on the route home, which I knew like the back of my hand, we drove an hour in the opposite direction.

I was a leader, yet there are times in life where I become a follower sometimes. When I did, that voice defiantly spoke up. Although it took a little more time to understand that just because everyone is doing it doesn't mean that I was supposed to do it too. There was another time when life showed up to show me, "Not you," as I handled one of my situations the way someone else would've.

CHAPTER 6

∞ Spreading My Wings ∞

I'm not exactly sure about the length of time I was at Mrs. BJ's house, but it was just what I needed. She is definitely a "fill in the blanks" person. I'm not 100% certain how things took place, but I do remember having an afternoon phone conversation with her, standing on the corner by Atwater's Café (a local black family-owned restaurant in the neighborhood). I talked to her in the phone booth, and I don't know if she could hear the despair in my voice or just pick up on the low vibrating frequency. Once again, divinity has shown her favor. So, I was now living with Mrs. BJ and her husband. Uncle Don is what I called him; he was an extraordinary man.

It was nice to have a man of stature in my life. The caliber of man he was had to be rare. Well, I know it was because I don't think any man had reminded me of my grandfather until I met him. Being at the house afforded me some time to ask myself some serious questions. Like, what do I want out of life, you know, things like that. I called this my man in the mirror experience.

Living with Mrs. BJ and her husband allowed me to rest my weary soul and settle my racing mind. I could face some of my ugly truths and had time to deal with some of the lies I told myself. I had now obtained a high school diploma for my online course that Mrs. BJ encouraged me to take. I also got a driver's license; Uncle Don made sure of that. I started working again at Checkers, nothing major, just to have some change in my pocket.

I laid low because I didn't want to get caught up in the whirlwind of life again; I wanted to do some soul searching. I remember Mrs. BJ settled in the living room, snuggled under her throw blankets, watching movies.

Kimmie would bring her son (my TT) Equilyes over on my days off so I could babysit. She used to bring him over in the morning when I had my apartment also on the days she had to go to work. I would just be getting off work because I did the 11 pm to 7 am shift at the nursing home. I was starting to miss him, but this was a better environment for him, so I could keep him through the night.

When I was off, he was there. One thing I liked about him, he was a big eater, so I would make him a full adult breakfast. He had everything! I remember one time; for some reason, he didn't want to eat my eggs. I called Kimmie almost in tears, and she laughed at me and said, "Girl get off my phone." Before she hung up, she was inquiring about our plans for that day because I usually found some kind of activity for us to do before I dropped him off for the night.

I began to tell her that it was never the straw that was the cause of the camel's back breaking in the first place. The straw is usually what causes the shift of the weight that was already there in the first place. The straw is always the cause, not the effect. My tears had nothing to do with the eggs was my point in all of that.

My mirror work and soul were starting to show themselves. I had to admit, I was feeling a little accomplished. This was the first time I felt this way in the adult world. I felt like I got there so quickly that I couldn't gain my footing. I couldn't secure a stable foundation. Life is hands down the best teacher. I now know life should not just be lived, but you have to live and learn.

I had a much better paying job at the Don Cesar, but I still worked at Checkers part-time. I found another family, my Checkers family. Tiffany and Tasha, they were sisters. Lawrence, Moe, Dasancer. Kimmie even got a part-time job working at Checkers. When we weren't at work, we would post up on Russell Street, at Tasha's apartment, or Ms. Twnett's house. Ms. Twnett was Lawrence's mother.

I had a full-time job and a part-time job. Life was starting to pick back up. I was allowing myself to get out of the house more. I was no longer just going to work and back home. I remember the nights we would go to The Dirty, which is a local bar in the city. We would meet at Jameeca's house so we could pregame before going in. Pregame, meaning we would drink and smoke before going into the club, so we didn't have to spend money on drinks in the club when we got there.

It felt like it was time to give life another try. Was I ready to leave the nest? Yeah, I'm sure that's how a baby bird feels right before the mama bird forces them to fly. It is actually a myth that mama birds push baby birds out of the nest in order to get them to fly. Rather, they coax them out of the nest to hustle their adolescence along. I was welcomed to stay as long as I needed, but the time had come to force adulthood along.

I had appreciated all the love and hospitality given to me while I was here, but I didn't want to wear out my welcome either. I felt like I was gaining my strength back, that I could leave the nest and learn to soar, not just fly this time. Flying would surely land me in the same place I just fought hard to pull myself out of. On the other hand, soaring would mean I was stronger, that I learned from my mistakes and was ready and capable of seeing life from a different view. I wasn't 100% certain that leaving the nest was best, but I knew 100% that I had everything I needed to soar on my own.

∞ *Sideline Winning* ∞

I was working my butt off, and I relive that as I write. This was the first time in my existence that I felt like I was working to help myself. Erica, too, in so many ways, was deciding to spread her wings as well. We talked some things over and decided to get an apartment together. Erica, her boyfriend, and I all moved in together. I had bought my first car, well, I was making payments on it.

I remember that there was a lot going on. Bills were coming in, I needed to make a payment to the lady I was buying the car from, and there were talks of going to New York with Auntie Patti. I was worried about money, but everything worked itself out. There was a bonus on my check, a referral bonus that gave me what I needed to pay my car off and take this trip.

This was the first of many flights to New York, but I was traveling as a first-time flyer to see my little cousins this time. They had gone to live with their father, so I hadn't seen them in years. As a matter of fact, I was living in the blue house when I saw them last. There was a knock on the door, and I opened it, and it was them. Surprised, yes, I was very surprised, because when I left home that afternoon for playing, and no one came to look for me, I assumed no one knew where I was. But the fact that I was looking at my cousins let me know that they found me; they just never came to retrieve me.

At the time, I was dating this guy named Brian, and before long, he decided to move in with me, well with us. I had gotten Erica a job at the Don also now. She was working in the Take 5 Kitchen, which was just a fancy word for the employee cafeteria. I ran a whole kitchen called The Beach Grill. It was an outside pool bar set-up kind of thing. For a few seconds, let me entertain you with the story of how I got this job running a whole kitchen.

When I got hired at the Don, it was for a stewarding position. Auntie Janet, Jerry's sister, had worked there and got me the job. Being in stewarding, you are responsible for the set-up of the banquet halls and any functions that they had planned for that day and set-up for the next day. I was responsible for making sure the correct number of plates, forks, and any other cutlery needed for the party or function was there. Since we were responsible for every dish and fork, that also included the new Beach Grill, which was currently in the process of opening up.

I got a call on my walkie talkie saying I needed to take the brand-new dishes down to the beach grill. I walked through the side door, and the fan blew my chef hat off my head. This was one of those industrial fans that kept the flies from coming in behind you as you come through the door. There was a guy standing on the opposite side of the tray line. I remember saying hello. I had a few words with him, dropped the dishes off, and said my goodbyes. I then headed back upstairs to the hotel.

By the time I got upstairs, Chris, who was my manager, had left a message saying that he wanted to see me in the office. I was slightly puzzled because I wondered what I could have possibly done wrong.

I hadn't even been there 90 days, and now I was being called into the office. When I got into the office, I sat down in the only black chair. The wheels were broken, so it wobbled.

I said, "Yes, sir, you wanted to see me."

He said it wasn't him who requested me. Chef Eric wanted to see me in his office. Now I was even more puzzled because Chef Eric was the Sous Chef of the whole hotel. He was responsible for creating the menus. I did not know at the time that the gentleman who I had seen when entering the Beach Grill was none other than Chef Eric. I went down to the Sea Porch because that's where his office was, and he told me that he wanted me to be the head chef of the Beach Grill.

Now, I had heard of this guy before. Naturally, he runs the show around here as far as making the full moves. But taking the dishes into the kitchen was our first brief encounter, and from that, Chef Sierra was born. Scripture writes it in Proverbs 18:16 as a powerful statement that reveals the answer: "A man's gift makes room for him." What you were designed to be known for is your gift.

I remember my afternoon phone conversation with Momma Duke; it was full of excitement and newness. I didn't know I had felt like that until I was writing this, that we were declaring that we were taking over the world. I felt at that very moment like I had done just that. Not the world in its entirety, but my world, space, thoughts, and emotions, which meant a lot from where I just came from.

I felt as if I had lost my sense of being, and with Chef Eric noticed all of my greatness, without me even telling him how cool I was or anything about me. He recognized it, and he saw it. He believed in what he saw, so why shouldn't I? I would call that a world takeover, wouldn't you? So, I started from the beginning, telling her what had happened, how these people were now going to trust me with knives in their kitchen. Like what were they thinking?

I always got excited when people trusted me to do tasks that I didn't even know I knew how to do. But, because they had enough faith in me to ask me to do it, I agreed, and I always came through. This was one of those moments. Unbeknownst to me, it wouldn't be the last time that my gift made room for me. The Don would bring about so many unique encounters and opportunities like learning new skills, friendships that bloomed into families, and much more.

I loved this new space that my gift had brought me to. I was presented with the opportunity to learn a new menu for the Beach Grill, but Chef Eric himself had to teach me. It was great, and part of me always wanted to do this. I went from the Steward Department to being Head Chef of my very own kitchen. When I received my Chef coat with my name on it and the black and white checkerboard pants, it was surreal. It was like the pinch that you asked for when you feel like you're dreaming.

This was all new for me but I was loving every moment of it. All of this happened in what should have been a 90-day probation. My status had changed, and my responsibilities were changing. The way I was starting to feel about myself had also changed. As time went on, I grew a bond with my servers, bartenders, and pool attendants crew. I mean, we had to work together, we had to be a team, I needed them just as much as they needed me in order to get the job done.

Sometimes on the weekends, usually Sunday mornings when the numbers would be low, I thought of them on my way to work. Yeah, a few things changed about this new world, but not my ability to just love, loving on people. I'd stop by the Publix right up the street and grab a few things so I could make all of them breakfast before they started their shift. Plus, I knew some of them were going to need it to help give them some substance in their belly to possibly help soak up what could still be floating around in their stomachs. On Sunday and Monday mornings, they were usually always talking about their partying from the night before. So, the least I could do was feed them.

Looks like my new world was going to be pretty interesting. It came with a sample of a Bloody Mary. I didn't see how this could taste any better with alcohol in it, but I guess it had something to do with helping a hangover. At least, that's what I assumed, because a few of those Sunday and Monday mornings, I watched while Heather would make them while stories were being told of the recaps of the previous night out on the town. Heather, you can say, was the leader of the pack. She was definitely the glue that was holding everybody together, like the mama bear or something.

Heather is now known as HQ. Yep, you guessed it. I am apart of another family. One that I would have never thought to find myself apart of, and not because she was a blonde-haired, blue-eyed girl; that wasn't the part that's hard to believe. The part that I'm speaking of is that this family came with three miniature-size dinosaurs. At least, that's what I considered them as, but the world knows them as Great Danes.

Delaney, our bundle of joy, when she was little, called them puppy dogs. I think she had some kind of insight on just how scared I was of these dogs. When I came over, and Dad would put the dogs out on the patio, she would grab my hand and say, "Come on, Auntie Sa-Sa, let's go see the puppy dogs."

I'm still uncertain if she was making fun of me or trying to help me get over my fear. She would just giggle, and I would be so serious in trying to explain to her that those were not puppy dogs but miniature dinosaurs. Heather's mom, at that moment, was battling cancer. I don't know what kind or what stage of cancer it was, not that it matters. Either way, whichever type it was, our feelings were the same #CancerSucks.

I remember her trying to encourage me when Heather was still pregnant. I believe Delaney was just born if my memory serves me correctly. But, I'm not totally sure, so we'll go with she was pregnant. I was concerned that Delaney would be concerned because I didn't look like the rest of her family. She's seventeen now, and I haven't experienced what my heart was so torn up about. I was being honest with myself on the hard truth I had to face as I'm aware of what it feels like. I had an experience of being treated differently because of the color of my skin.

As Heather's due date approached, I grew more and more concerned that she was going to feel the same way. The only lesson I got from that is that racism is clearly taught to people and to our children. I'll get back to that (perhaps in another book).

Christmas parties and trips to Busch Gardens were my favorite time of the year. Let's talk about the day the hotel sends all the employees to Busch Gardens as their appreciation for our service. It was lunchtime, and if you wanted a free meal, that was provided for you. We had to meet at a certain time, so a few of us from the Beach Grill decided to head there as we were now hungry. I remember walking in and laughing. I got my tray and headed over to the table where everyone was sitting.

I looked up, and I saw my father sitting at a table with a little girl who looked exactly like me; this was definitely a shock. Talk about being caught off guard. I'm not sure at this time how long it had been since the last time I saw him, but I definitely wasn't prepared for this! I walked right past both of them. Honestly, I wanted to act like I didn't know him. So, I kept walking to the table and sat down with the others. Although I tried to hold them back, the tears were coming down my face before I knew it.

Everyone was uncertain about what was going on because just a few minutes ago, we had just come into the building cracking jokes and laughing about things. I couldn't just say anything. I mean, they could clearly see it was something. So, I shared with them that my father was sitting over there at the table with his little girl, who looks exactly like a smaller version of me. Very few people at this table had ever heard me mention my father, and you already know I don't like to let people see me crying.

Despite this feeling of being suffocated from these off-guard emotions, I wiped my face, and I decided to walk over. Of course, he recognized me, I was his child, and I looked just like him. I pulled up a chair and sat down across from him. What was hard to swallow was this little girl had this proud look on her face because she was sitting with her father, and she should feel exactly that way.

I'm not certain how I internally processed all of this and how we were able to wrap our minds around exactly what we were experiencing. At some point, I had to get up from the table, heartbroken as I walked away. Not with the proud look of this little girl sitting next to him, rather with the feelings of being a stranger and having been short-changed again on the whole father-daughter experience, yet again. I can't remember at this moment if I knew that his wife worked at the Don with me or this was my first time it was being made known.

I guess it really didn't matter because nothing changed after that moment, even with his knowledge of his daughter, whom he hadn't seen in quite some time, working at the same place his wife did.

Nothing changed. Even with his wife knowing he had a child who worked at the same place she did, nothing changed.

I remember a time, sitting on the back dock waiting for my ride, a white car was in the distance, and I heard voices. Kasandra, my dad's wife, was one of those voices I heard. She walked by me down the ramp and walked her way over to the car I saw sitting in the distance. She brought my attention to it because it's the car she got in. I looked up, and I could recognize the gentleman driving was my father. She got in the car, closed the door, and they drove off.

I couldn't understand this. It was really puzzling to me because she definitely knew who I was when she walked past me and got in the car with my dad. For her, as a mother, to not make sure my father and I were aware of each other was mind-blowing to me. I mean, she went home and laid down next to him that night, and got up the next day and came to work, and spoke to me as if nothing about her own actions disturbed her. How, as a woman, as a mother, could she be ok with herself?

CHAPTER 7

♥ You Didn't Put in on This ♥

Mom was now staying with me; it was straight-up spiritual warfare. My car had become my altar, my safe place. Still to this day, I find myself sitting there, gathering my thoughts or letting go of some. Our spirits being at war is a great way to explain the experience. When Momma Duke was on drugs and drinking, she could be abusive, physically and verbally. She had gotten better but would still verbally put me down. I had to tell myself she didn't get the right to do that!

All that we have become is amazing, regardless of what she did or didn't do. Duke was trying to tear down the woman I had become, no ma'am. I had a 2-bedroom apartment, and she was able to have her own room. I would still go to work and come home.

I remember this time—it had to be around Christmas—I bought the soft peppermint tasting candies that I remember my grandmother buying when I was little. So, I bought this candy in memory of her, and when I went into the fridge and all the candy was gone, I was devastated. I was angry and way past upset, but more so at this woman who did not put in on them. I've fought so hard to be where we were now, so for this woman to be here in my place, putting me down, making fun of me, was too much. I remember her actually saying one day, "I'm your mama; I can do what I want."

That wasn't true either. Just because you're my mother doesn't give you the right to mistreat me. Back to the candy, I was standing at the refrigerator, and I realized all this candy that I had intentionally bought for myself to remind me of my grandmother was gone with no regard. She was just looking at it as a piece of candy, the idea that you would eat something that you didn't pay for.

I remember going to my room and closing the door, and she came through the door behind me. As I sat on the edge of the bed with my head down, she said, "I bet you're in here crying, aren't you?" Just to torment me because she knew how sensitive I was. I looked up at her and stared her in the face and said no, I'm not. She turned around and closed the door behind her. The moment the door closed, the Nile River was unleashed from my eyes.

Even though this was a struggle, I was determined to honor my mother so that my days might be long, like the scripture reads. I was able to do just that. I had never raised my voice or fixed my mouth to say a bad word. Never would I let her see me cry. I never put her down either. All the efforts I made were so that she could heal and live a healthy, drug-free life.

I am proud to say that she went on to go to Florida Career College to graduate as a medical assistant. She is currently my superhero, the person who has taught me how to budget money as well as my comedian, my road trip partner, and my mother. She now has her own apartment where she and my stepdad live.

I find myself needing her now, more than I thought I did way back then. So, once again, divine timing proves itself. Now drug and alcohol-free, she's one of my favorite people today. They say the apple doesn't fall far from the tree, and had you asked me when I was younger, I would have told you there was no way we could have so much in common. But, I see myself in her, and she has taught me so much. I'm glad she decided to live. Who would have thought I would need her more now.

♥ *What's Love Got to Do with It? (EVERYTHING)* ♥

I didn't really have hopes and dreams for the adult me. I knew I would have a job, just wasn't sure doing what. I wanted a three or four-bedroom home, although I did not want children. I remember setting a goal to have it by the time I was 25. I made money, but I was so busy loving on everybody else that what I wanted took the back burner. I'm not really sure when this started for me, but I noticed I was definitely in a cycle of putting everyone else's concerns before my own.

It seemed I took a silent oath of some sort to protect and serve. I figured that loving them would create a shield around them, and I was saving them from all the pains that I experienced. In fact, at this point, if you were to ask me what made me happy, I'd say making others happy. Now I think about it, that was the only thing that I could say I got my happiness from. How sad does that sound?

This mindset produced my perspective. Indeed, it was the very thing that held me back from flourishing.

I've come to realize that I had a complex with love, and because of it, I subsequently taught people, but more importantly myself, how to treat me. This resulted in an off and on long-distance relationship, more off than on. That and so much more because of this complex. As I'm now able to have a closer look, when did I start facing my truth and my lies? When I told myself about love? I've hidden behind other people's greatness so I could remain complacent with myself. I found accountability in being there for others but had not learned to be accountable to myself.

We finally got married in August 2016. Let's say I again found a way not to listen to my voice within. I ignored every bright red flag I saw and made pretty little trees out of them to go with this picture I was choosing to see. I'm not saying the two of us should not have been married, but what I'm saying is that my voice, my spirit, God, whoever—somebody was trying to tell me something. I should have at least addressed their concerns. Greg was just as passive as I was.

I knew if we didn't pull things from the root, they were surely going to sprout back up. Here went everything, a new battle with the old complex of love. While trying to see the new way that I loved myself, I was trying to teach every person, place, and thing how to love me as well. Yes, the price for this experience was going to cost me everything.

There go those dots again, connecting themselves. Even with my eyes full of tears, I can see them. This picture I had painted, with pretty little trees, was fading. The dots now revealed that there was a picture in this picture. You can also see it like scripture has written, having a ram in the bush, or a lesson to be learned. Seeing the good out of the bad.

Who would have thought that the sign I purchased from the gift shop at work would play a tremendous part in my story? The sign read, "Find Joy in the Journey." I remember grabbing it one day. It called to me, and this time I listened. I bought it, not yet realizing that I was on the most important journey of my life.

Finding Sierra

I had thought that I had been here before, but I was sadly mistaken. This was truly the threshing floor, the place where all things were about to be determined. The place where the real Sierra, the authentic Sierra, would have to stand up.

Sierra is no longer allowing anyone to walk all over her. Sierra is learning to love herself and accept the cards that have been placed in front of her. No longer is she using family battles or traumas as a crutch. She is walking on her own path and plan for her life. Sierra is strong, and nothing can disturb her peace of mind. She is focused. One thing that remains the same in her, no matter what is her loyalty, kind heart, selflessness, and love. Only now, she shares this with people that want to build her up and not tear her down.

What's love got to do with it? **Everything** is my answer, in my Tina Turner voice, because it all starts with you loving you. It's easy to say I still have a complex with love, but this time I won't be getting the short end of the stick.

CHAPTER 8

∞ "40" I'm Coming Out ∞

I was in a place that I had avoided for a very long time. A place that I had also protected myself from going to. This place I'm talking about is on the inside of me. As I can boldly say, my spirit had given me instructions that my healing was going to come from people, places, and things. I knew this time I had to be my first line of defense. I knew this time I could not be that version of myself ever again. I knew this time that we would have to take a different route.

I knew this time that if I wanted different results, permanent results, I would have to do things differently. I'm able to talk to people now without crying. Some say they knew I would make it out ok.

On the other hand, I tried to explain to them how I was worried about who I would be when all the dust settled. My kingdom had been breached, and the enemy was in my space, love, being the enemy, but this time, it was my love of self that had decided to take charge. The thing that we kept out was actually the thing that saved us, but it had to come from me. In order to get out, I had to go in. I could imagine that scene from *Ghostbusters*, where they would capture the ghost and take them back to the vault.

There's an episode where all the ghosts escaped, and they had to get them back in. I was currently living this with all my past traumas. All the things that I had covered up, all the times I wanted to scream and never screamed. All the things that I needed to express and never said anything. They were now out of my vaults, free of my fortified Kingdom, haunting me, and not in a way to scare me.

Yeah, I was definitely petrified, but in a way, they were too. They wanted answers and clarity. Much I did, and I realized this time, I had no place to hide them. I was going to have to face all these feelings and emotions. The good, the bad, and the ugly in different parts of myself as I embarked on this journey.

It has taken forgiveness of self and a brave girl to arrive at this present place within myself. I'm sure to some, I look the same, and they might beg to differ that nothing has changed about me. This change has nothing to do with my outward being, looks, job, income, car, or where I live. Moreover, my inward change that has taken place has definitely allowed me to get to know myself again in ways I didn't even know lived on the inside of me. It was like meeting long lost parts of yourself.

My walls are down, my ghosts are out, and we are unlearning to relearn. We are being intentional about addressing my traumas and emotions that I had covered up. I did a lot of pretending on certain pains not existing. This is what we are coming out of, the lower version of myself. We are coming out of that place we once took refuge in. We are coming out of the old thoughts of what we were created for. We are coming out of feeling inconsistent in my own skin, and we are coming out of that thought of not feeling love.

∞ *Blue isn't just a color;*
it's an attitude ∞

Things were personal this time around! There's a place where scripture says, "Old things are passed away and behold all things made new." I was in that place that now craved this newness. I was a blank canvas now that everything was out of the bag, and I was at the end of myself. I realized that I had been trying to wake myself up for this for quite some time. I'm up! I'm up! I'm wide awake now. I'll never be a sleeping beauty again. I was going to make certain of it. I've heard the story of the wolf, where the grandson asked the grandfather about which wolf was stronger, and the grandfather's reply was, whichever wolf you feed the most.

Self was no longer mastering me, and I was doing what it took to no longer waste my energy feeding the (dead) negative parts of me. Here's another way to look at it. This one isn't a story; they are true facts. We are not that different from plants; think about why you should cut off dead leaves.

1. To free up nutrients and encourage new growth
2. To prevent the spread of disease or pests
3. To improve health and appearance

Dead leaves leech nutrients from the plant. Removing them allows the remaining, healthy foliage to receive more nutrients and improves the plant's life. Although it may seem simple enough, there's more to it than just snipping off those leaves. Scripture describes it as being pruned so you might bear more fruit. Consider how much of the leaf is dying and how removing the damaged parts properly allows the plant to maintain its life.

I could now fully, with a sound mind, determine what was best for me. I knew that I didn't just have to take what life was throwing at me. I don't recall who I was talking to, but I remember saying assertively that this time I was going to be the one calling the shots! That for here on out, I was going to tell life how this game was going to go. I had no control over the cards that were dealt, but I had full control over the way I played my hand. I put my game face on...Royal flush, baby!!!!

I had spent enough time being trapped in myself. While I was in the midst of my transformation, there was another bomb dropped again. This was so out of left field that it took the whole family off guard. My phone was ringing as I sat in the driver's seat of my car. When I finally got the phone out of my purse, it was my cousin Talisha. She was asking if I had gotten a call from Patti or my momma about Kimmie (my sister, cousin, friend) passing away.

"No one called me," I told her.

I said, "Let me call my mom." So I hung up and called Momma Duke, she answered.

Sounding half asleep, I said, "Ma, has Auntie Patti called you?"

She said, "No." I didn't tell her why I had asked cause I knew this was some big joke.

As I sighed with relief, she said, "Hold on, Patti calling me."

"No, Ma, you talk to Patti," I said. "I'll call you back."

My head dropped, my heart stopped, and tears started to fill my eyes. Feeling my heart become heavy, I still couldn't help but smile. I realized I had been lowkey channeling her energy all day. I started to smile because I noticed what I was wearing for the occasion, these lime green pants I had bought when we had gone shopping in New York.

Some of the family had decided to link up seven months prior to spend some family time together and create memories. Kimmie was always my hype man, always boosting me up, which was just her getting me to appreciate myself. It was Saint Patrick's Day, and I was downtown with KK and some of her friends. The pants were so lime green that Darleen, Kimmie's little sister, said, "When you wear them, I'm going to be able to see you all the way from New York." Yes, that's just how bright green they were.

This was so unexpected. This section should really be left blank because there aren't any words that I could have typed to explain what I was feeling. This was my first sister. I remember I used to sit on the toilet seat for her just to warm it up. I love that I wanted to do that for her; it makes me smile. I could feel the essence of that little girl looking out the window. Love is definitely one of my superpowers. This is my first cousin, and at one point before my grandma dropped the bomb, my sister was the only sister I had.

Patti always dressed us alike, her in blue, me in pink. I wanted nothing to do with this feeling at this moment; this would have been a perfect reason to disconnect. This could have been a chance where I could have been nominated again for the greatest actress of the year. We were not going to let it go down like that; I had overcome too much.

I strived to get this far. How dare I give up on myself now when I could see all of these amazing things about myself that I could never see before. I have good problems now. I look in the mirror, and I'm often saddened by how I could not see just how majestic and complex I was.

Just like that, we shifted the energy from that place of pain. I looked at it head-on since I was learning to channel my energy. I was learning that just because I felt crappy doesn't mean I have to lower myself to match that energy. I learned that just because It feels like I can't, I still can. I'm telling myself I can a lot more nowadays by pushing past my surface level, which is my emotions.

We forget that we are spiritual beings in the flesh. You see more clearly when your reactions to a situation have been processed and not just felt. I'm learning a lot about what they told us we should not do is actually the very thing that we should be doing. You're darn right, it was personal this time. We had forfeited so many things, and we didn't even try most of the time.

I just automatically counted myself out. Not this time around, I won't stand in my own way any longer, hence why I hogtied and duct-taped that version of myself and put her in the corner. I'm learning to listen to my navigational system a lot more. I was cutting off every dead thing that aided in the (Made Up Stuff) belief of who I was not. No more just living life on the surface, riding every roller coaster of emotion. Instead, I took that feeling and turned it into an expression by learning from it instead of just feeling it. Blue has become a characteristic of courage, not just an emotion.

#BlueLipsDontCare

∞ *Pretty Flowers Grow from Dark places* ∞

Finding joy in being my best, most magical self was now the plan and the number one priority. Being out of the box was coming with less and less petrifying thoughts and days of anxiety. This was good in itself, but I had to ask myself the real question because I didn't have it in me to take another trip around the mountain of inward uncertainty. The question I had to ask myself was, "What do you do now to stay out?"

I knew I couldn't be that version of myself ever again. I was so angry at myself for allowing myself to be ok with the life I settled for, the treatment I took from people just to try to show them I love them. A big revelation that helped bring me to this evolution was that it was ok to be intentional with my life and not just accept what life dishes out. I'm certain that my mindset of "good things come to those that wait" played a part. I heard a flipside to my motto that said, "Those that feel good things come to those that wait are probably still waiting." Ouch, yeah, that was a hard pill for me to swallow cause at one point, that was my motto.

Love didn't always come from the people that I wanted it from. But, I always had people that loved me with no problem. The problem existed because I didn't love myself. I didn't feel like I deserve it either.

I get now why people love me cause I am lovable.

∞ CHAPTER 9

♥ Self Planting Seeds ♥

I remember I was very intentional with myself at this stage in my life. I knew I needed to start telling myself positive things on a daily basis to counteract the M.U.S I had been telling myself for years. Words do matter! Very much so they do. Not only do they matter, but your words also become like the paint to a paintbrush. They will create a picture that you'll start living by. Words do matter. It would be nice to talk to the person that came up with the saying, "Sticks and stones will break my bones, but words will never hurt me." I would like to ask this person what they meant by those words. I know what I think when I say them. Yeah, I'm definitely curious about the meat and potatoes of the statement. At different times in my life, I've been able to see it from several different perspectives. Words do matter, especially your words.

> "Their words might hurt,
> but it's your words that changes
> THE WHOLE NARRATIVE!!!!!"

Define narrative: a spoken or written account of connected events; a story.

This is what it has come down to, by any means necessary. At the cost of everything that is not aligned and goes against my greatness, including the lower vibrating parts of self. I made it my business to water myself with these six seeds daily.

- *Sierra, I celebrate all of you (everything you are & everything you're not)*
- *Sierra, be willing to invest in you (know your worth, then add tax)*
- *Sierra, give yourself permission (to be a better version of yourself)*
- *Sierra, stop living like you don't know your truth (confront your traumas)*
- *Sierra, get out of your own way (stop sabotaging your greatness)*
- *Sierra, you are responsible for yourself (be your first line of defense)*

I titled them self-planting for a reason. This was going to further teach me how to invest in myself. Deliberately planting words in my mind that once watered and cultivated will produce a bountiful harvest.

❤ *Sometimes the issue –*
Is U ❤

Have you ever stopped to think that you were your own problem, like, this whole time you were getting in your own way? That the issue just might be you? I mean, think about it, with all the things that have transpired in your life, what's the common denominator? The common denominator is U. I know it's a hard thought to consider. Let me speak for myself, so I'm going to talk about me and not you. But, if at some point you are truly seeking self-elevation, consider that the things around you are a reflection of who you are. We're like mirrors. We reflect, and so that's what we attract. Dress up this flesh all you want. Wear every mask you can find, but you will always attract what's within.

Evaluate your circle; we are the company we keep. But, don't forget those three fingers that are pointed back at you. It's definitely a road you're going to have to travel down at some point. I was tired of getting in my own way. I was tired of making the same mistakes over and over again. If I had to go around this mountain of uncertainties while listening to my insecurities whisper to me, I didn't think I could survive another round of it. I told my therapist I was afraid of who I would become, now able to feel the pain, of everything I could no longer run from.

~ 133 ~

Even in writing this, there are reminders of how I constantly got in my way. I've always had my internal voice speaking to me. If I had only taken heed of that voice that was always trying to lead me in the right direction. So, full of self-doubt, I just chose not to listen to my natural GPS. That voice was me speaking up, wanting what was best for me. It was only doing what it was designed to do, help steer me in the right direction, but we didn't listen, and we still have trouble listening to this small, still voice.

I could hear other people's GPS's (greatness) speaking louder than my own, allowing me to find security in their final destination. I was never seeking out my own, but hiding in the shadows of their greatness instead.

Lisa Nichols, a famous motivational speaker, said something that was paradigm-shifting.

"I'm not extraordinary; you don't get off the hook. You don't get to be let off the hook. I'm an ordinary woman who chooses every day to make one more extraordinary decision."

♥ *Taking the Trash Out* ♥

Taking Sierra out of Sierra so I can get into Sierra has been ministering to me for years. I had no idea how far the knowledge of this concept would take me, just how deep down the rabbit hole I would go. I was in church with my now ex-husband when we were dating. Before Pastor McKnight started to preach, he usually addresses the congregation by telling a story of some sort. You either got a good laugh or a good spanking by the time the message was over. That day, it was a spanking, and from that spanking, this concept was birthed.

I understood it completely. I made it personal and applied it. That, my dear reader, is what you call OVER STANDING. The story was referring to these bottles that he was filling up with oil to pass out to the congregation. Personalizing the story helped make it stick, and it has definitely helped me get where I am today. It has helped me not to continue to lie to myself, and it has helped me realize and accept that I was the common denominator.

The most freeing overstanding was that I have options. For a long time, I didn't know I had the option to change things. I didn't know I had the option to see things differently. I didn't know I had the option to feel differently about what my flesh might be telling me. I didn't know I had the freedom I speak of.

An application of understanding your life is called overstanding, using that concept to make you better. To aid in the elevation of yourself is what we call an inner-standing. Anyway, he went on to say that he was in the process of filling up these bottles (it was those little bottles that have the bubble stuff in them that you would get at weddings), and the spirit spoke to him and told him not to fill the bottles up all the way. He said Spirit continued saying that if you fill the bottles up all the way, there would be no room for me to get in the bottle! I'm sure his sermon was extremely good for that day, but I don't recall any of it. That was my only take away.

We, you, are the problem, Sierra get out of your way! My words will do this part no justice, so from my actions, you'll just have to see that there's a wonderful change that has come over me, and we can be our authentic self. That amazing being you were divinely created to be hit me like a freight train; it hit me like Ike did Tina in the back of that limousine. Remember, you are responsible for your physical health, mental health, and, most importantly, your expansion growth. Stop allowing people, including yours truly, to dump their trash in your freshly watered grass.

When I come to think about it, the process of getting out of my own way started when I didn't even know it was starting. Since hearing that message, my life has not been the same. I was manifesting a new version of myself. I was experiencing life within my life. I was expanding my brain.

I was walking into caves deep within that had been harvesting parts of myself. I was on what felt like a treasure hunt to discover those parts, but it was scary. It was full of unexpected things like Indiana Jones in *The Temple of Doom* when he discovers a treasure deep in some dark cave.

Never knowing how precious it could be, there was definitely more of me I was becoming aware of while growing in my self-awareness. I was learning what I like and what I did not like. I was learning my dos and don'ts, wills, and wants. I now had a sense of direction, and I no longer felt lost in this life.

Once I became aware of self, things became a lot clearer, so it improved my focus, and I wanted to live. I felt like I had a right to live. I knew how to use what I once considered a weakness as my strength. I was more motivated and driven than I had ever been.

I've never been one to give up easily. I found great resilience. I knew why I had to do this, and I was the reason why. Not even in death did I consider myself worthy. When having thoughts of suicide, I remember the only reason I did not kill myself was thinking about who would be there for my mother? Who was going to be there for my sister? Who was going to stop Precious from fighting somebody? Not even in considering taking my own life did I see the value of my life. All this time, my inner strength was my solid foundation on which I could stand.

CHAPTER 10

∞ D. A. R. E 2 Be ∞

I remember my spirit telling me one thing, that everything I needed to recover from this dark place was going to come from within me. To rise from this fall, my help wasn't going to come from my old ways of doing things. As self-destruction was one of the ways, it had to come to an end. It was time to pull out the big guns, search and destroy every low vibrating part of myself. I would have to do something differently if I wanted different results this time around.

I was being crushed, I was being made again, and I knew I wasn't about to put my new wine in old vessels. I was in a place I had unknowingly avoided all my life. I was alone with me, myself, and I. I was taking this time to get to know us intentionally. We had done everything to prevent this moment from happening, even the unaware willingness to die, which stifled my growth and my love of self. It also dimmed my light and didn't allow me to live out my purpose.

It seems I was willing to live and die to a life where I listened to everything else but myself again and again. So, today, we were taking a stance to dare to be us. I found out that I could take my power back by having knowledge of self and manifest the life I want with limitless power. Being the source of this power, I could dare the real Sierra to please stand up, please stand up.

I DARE myself to be true, authentic, and unapologetically SMC. This would be the hardest thing I could do, which I never thought I would do, so I remembered an acronym from back in school. It was a slogan they used to help you say no to drugs. I then came up with my own acronym to help me remember to stay on the course of being my authentic self.

- D = **Die** – to the lower version of self, **detach** from everything that drains you.
- A= **Align** – yourself with people who look like you, **accept** everything about you, everything.
- R= **Relearn** – your importance of being created, **resolve** any and all unforgiveness of self and others.
- E= **Evolve** – from all that you went through, learn from it, and with that knowledge, **elevate** yourself to rise higher than any situation or distraction.

I D. A. R. E you to be a better you.
You want better, do better by you
"A Better You = A Better Me."
"A Better Me = A Better You."

∞ *I am Who I Have Been Waiting On* ∞

Now that I had a knowledge of self that saturated my love of self, which bloomed into respect of self, I could no longer be the old version of myself. The one thing that aided in my grief would be the very thing that kept me free. I had a lot of practice at being loving, caring, and giving of myself wholeheartedly to others. This only molded me into the person I needed to be that would set myself free.

Life has messed around, and let me find out that I'm the key!! I was the last dot on this canvas to be connected so that the masterpiece could be revealed. I was the missing piece of my puzzle to complete me. I was the version of myself that would unlock or kick down every door that stood in the way of me being the creator of my divinity. I became my very own superhero!!

So, as I continue to grow into this new me, I always have to reflect on the many things that helped me become me. Now that I know where the only true power lies, I can only hold myself accountable for my peace and self-worth. It is a process, and I am learning to love what it is, cause the results speak for themselves. I've been part of many processes, and this one has presented the most tangible and timely results.

I was being intentional with the direction that I invested my energy. I've always invested in others, and now it is mine and mine alone to harness and use. We have to continue to tell ourselves these things because no one will remind you of your purpose or power. No one but the individual in the mirror, and sometimes, even you can be stubborn to yourself.

It's a beautiful thing to unlock so much of myself without having a fear of what I may experience while doing so. Yes, there will always be scary moments, but the moment doesn't last forever; it only lasts as long as you allow yourself to live in that moment. I am learning that I am the timekeeper, so I am the controller of the time spent at every moment, great or small. This allows me to enjoy every moment because the only thing that defines a good or bad moment is the weight of the thought that you put on it.

So, I will continue to show up for myself with no hesitation intentionally. Freely living and giving unto me the things I used to wait around for others to give. I've come to realize that it was not the obstacles in my way, though some perhaps intentionally put in my way, which slowed my progress. It was the obstacles within myself, the ones covered, created, or placed there from childhood traumas, that kept me bound.

The thought haunted me, feeling that this was all I was to be or become and the only thing that I was to feel. I was finally able to break down some of those things, to see the light on the horizon, but also for me to finally know that I am more than the feelings of defeat and despair.

Battling with those things for so long has only added to my magical self. It has allowed me to see that I am truly more than I ever gave myself credit for. It has given me the opportunity to know myself in ways that I never knew even existed

My brain is being turned on, and I am using it in ways I've never done before, ways I never knew I could. I love the way my brain works. I can picture the gears turning inside my head, like in a cartoon when they're showing that someone is thinking. I love it; it excites me that I am using it! There is a saying, a mind is a terrible thing to waste. I now have an over and inner standing of what they meant by that. It is proven that we can waste our thoughts on so many other things that are not relevant, not even important.

This is where some common sayings come from, like stinky thinking. It is all that BS I talked about, that made-up stuff I discussed. A mind is a terrible thing to waste, and you don't have an eternity to use it. We never know when our time is going to be up. I was no longer willing to take this chance. I was no longer willing to waste my mind on stinky thinking. No more of casually waking up. I was no longer going to wake up and leave my dreams on my pillow.

I'm going to move every and anything out of my way. I discovered a big part of that, every and anything was me. It is evident for me now that divinity was telling me that I was bigger than this box I was convinced existed. I mean, hell, even Stevie Wonder could see. The world even played its part in painting this picture that I needed to evolve into another person (my higher self) in order to achieve my dreams. I'm not waking up to a mediocre life because I know I have the ability to affirm myself. I now know to be intentional with myself. My dreams will no longer be left behind on my pillow, but yet rather made room for, to give them a chance to bloom. Taking it out of my mind, putting it in my possession.

Behind the Pages

*T*his section shows hardcore evidence that I am using my brain in so many different ways. I LOVE IT. I thought of the behind the pages section much like a screenwriter does when they leave movie clips of some of the things that happened behind the scenes. This is my rendition of that, just for a book, which is why this section is titled Behind the Pages. This section is snippets of thoughts and emotions of what was going on behind the pages while I was trying to write this book and a few testimonies from random people who noticed a change in me.

I gave them headings so you can have a footnote on what was taking place. It's not a movie, so you can't see it, but this allows you to use your imagination. I was excited when this thought came about because I wrote this book in real-time while dealing with real-life shit while still trying to be my real self. So, I thought it was important to share these encounters with you. We often say we're waiting on the perfect time, but that is never going to happen. There is no such thing as a perfect time. I do believe there is such a thing as divine timing and that, my dear reader, you have no control over. Behind the pages reveals real-life things while trying to do real-life stuff. You can do it! Get out of your way and stop making excuses is the point I'm trying to make.

Stepping Over Fear

Even here and now, I sit, wiping tears from my eyes. I've been up since 4:30 this morning with the excitement of knowing I am writing a book, and yet it is now 1:38 PM. We are once again making excuses to do everything but sit down and do what we are actually internally excited about doing. Does this self-habit-forming behavior ever go away? Is this just something that we will continue to take ourselves through? And yet, still, I smile because I am finally here writing my book.

I think I'm just scared to tell my story. Why? We can do this. Give what you lived through, what you experienced, a voice.

I felt like we had superpowers because everyone had no problem talking to me. I love the self-talks I have been having lately. But, I'm reminded that I was just a little girl who needed guidance. A little girl that felt like she couldn't call anybody. You never had to. We will do this; we will conquer our demons and wear our scars like wings.

We will continue to wrestle with every thought that is contrary to my being and who I am divinely created to be. I am made up of everything I am and everything I'm not.

D.A.R.E 2 B

While writing this book, today's date is 9/16/2020, and the time is 4:05 PM. I ask myself, who do I think I am? What makes me think that I can write a book? I was no longer taking my own junk or believing in my own lies, so I said, what makes you think that we cannot write this book? I was running too fast in the direction, of my greatness of being My Best, Most Magical Self to even slow myself down with that (M.U.S) made up stuff

I made room for this moment; it took a minute to realize what was actually happening. My forehead started heating up. My heart was racing, and my feet and hands started sweating. One of us was like, it's happening! A strong feeling of awkwardness engulfed me. After a long moment of silence, I couldn't see anything, but I could feel everything. This was anticipated, an encounter I knew I needed to have in order to complete this book.

I admit I wanted to get this book done quickly. I mean, it's my story; no one else can tell it better than me. It wasn't going to take me that long to write it out. In order to complete the book, this encounter was necessary because there was a side of my story that only she could tell. I was at the core of myself. I was face to face with the little girl in me. When I realized what was

taking place, I was able to hit the audio and record button on the computer, and this is some of that reunion. I didn't change any of the words; I just added punctuation to help bring a better understanding of the conversation.

We are sorry, we had it all wrong. We are sorry for not knowing the answers, and we are sorry that we didn't figure it out sooner. I am sorry that we left you behind. We only thought we were doing what's best for you. We thought we were protecting you when actually, we're the ones our abandonment issues come from. It just hit me, it's not funny we can feel our pain now, and we couldn't feel it before.

We aren't telling her who we are. Do you have a right to know just how amazing you are? Do you have a right to know what you've overcome?

Sierra, I am part of you. It's OK to pat yourself on the back, Sierra. We celebrate all of you. See here, Sierra, be willing to invest in yourself, know your worth, and then add tax. Sierra, give yourself permission to be your best, most magical self.

Sierra, stop loving like you don't know your truth. Confirm your troubles 'cause my truth don't care about your feelings. Sierra, get out of your way. No, it isn't fair, but it's also not fair that we treat ourselves a certain way because Sierra, you are responsible for you. You're responsible for taking your own trash out, and trash turns into my first line of defense.

Here I am, oh my goodness! Oh, my goodness! Oh, my goodness! Something so deep just connected together. It actually feels like I'm getting an electrical surge right now. The reasoning is kicking in. I'm telling my younger self that she will no longer have to be afraid that she will be so proud of the woman she's become. I've told so many other people to come forward. I try to encourage them, uplift them.

I remember doing a video saying that I needed to start practicing what I preached, and it's funny cause normally, when people make that threat, they're referring to someone else, not themselves. Then, I was personally in a negative state. You needed to show me in a believing way because younger me is not believing what the adult me is saying. On the other hand, I am telling myself this is slightly different because I've always shown a good judge of character as far as my actions, just not to myself.

What I am referring to are the words that I have given to others to encourage them. I have always displayed it in my actions. Just not to myself. Again, this is the very problem that added up to the reason we are fighting this fight.

Stepping over fear, stepping over those made-up things, and you know we just heard the adult Sierra assure the young Sierra that everything is going to be ok. We are going to be all right; we got us! You have an amazing family, like so much is happening, and I'm so glad I'm able to share with you. I'm so glad to be able to be in a place where I can be myself, which doesn't make me feel like I'm in competition with anything.

We're not in competition with my lower self's frequency either, so it's a great place to be. I'm glad that we continued to have fought when we fall, so we can make it here. I'm excited, and I'm proud to say all of us have found joy in this journey. Being aligned feels like home. Never will I allow such a disconnect again where I refer to myself in a plural context. 😊😌

Nothing about that was made up. That moment was REAL! So real that shortly after I got a call, I don't recall who, at the moment, I was talking to. But they stopped me mid-sentence and pointed out that I considered myself in a single plural context.

I explained how I would talk in third, second, and sometimes what I felt was fourth person. I said, "I," which I had not done for quite some time. The first person I verbally spoke to after this amazing connection recognized it. It was an instant change, one I didn't have to run and tell of because they recognized it. It doesn't get any more real than that.

At the same time, I was convincing myself, especially after that encounter, to go workout with the girls. I wasn't feeling much like a winner at that point. A part of being this amazing person I told my child self about when I was changing, that not going was not an option. This moment was so real readers. I'm certain these emotions were coming from separate places (know thy self). We are not feeling blue today. I put on my shirt that day that said #IWIN to redirect my energy.

PS: God Mother, I found the people with hearts like mine; they do exist. There are people with hearts like me! They are called MU (Manifest University). We are manifesting a life of greatness while overstanding to inner-stand the path that has led us all here. We have joined ourselves together as a tribe. We are getting out of our way to allow us to all grow into being self-sustaining African individuals that help ensure no one's fire goes out so that we can burn up our paths to destiny. Creating a black excellence combustion that will be seen for generations to come.

Disclaimer

The exciting part about writing this book is that I can now joyfully say,

"THIS BOOK AINT ABOUT YOU!"

I can see clearly now that the rain is gone. What didn't kill me only expanded me. It changed my perspective on life itself, not just the hand I was dealt. I have no ill will towards the people, places, or things I wrote about in this book. I don't believe in happenstance, yet rather, all things occur for a reason.

I've fought my hardest battles and overcame my toughest obstacles, which were SELF. I speak these words from a healthy, healed, and whole space. Life is to be experienced, not just lived. I know my truth, and I love myself, no longer through others' opinions and eyes.

In giving authentic truth to my voice, I realized my power, peace, and truth comes from within. I've unlearned, to relearn, which birthed overstanding. That lead to inner-standing, allowing clarity to be my GPS on this journey.

Afterword

What's next?? For the first time, I can relate to the sky is the limit. And the beauty of this is that I not only now believe it to be true, but I can also feel it. An alarm screams of urgency, the ringing in my soul has sounded out like the clock striking 12, on the night Cinderella went to the ball.

Instead of my carriage turning back into a pumpkin, destiny says it is time! Old things are passed away. Behold all things new.

What's next, you asked? You can expect me to live my best, most magical life. Doing speaking engagements, mentoring, becoming a life expansion coach, and creating multiple streams of income.

It is important for me to continuously be a light. I love on people through my words, thoughts, and deeds. I've found myself, and I've boldly answered destiny's call.

Call to action

Want to know what Sierra was doing
before she became an Author??

Here's a link to some footage,
where you can hear and see for yourself.

https://youtube.com/channel/
UCijXE0SFgEFp13WJY8N4ZcQ

Watch, Download, Share

**FREE PDF of the six self-planted seeds,
...d into affirmations for daily BLOOMING**

... am" can be powerful. In fact, they are said to be the most
...ful words in the world. They are powerful enough that anything
...wing the two words can be manifested. So, it's important that
...u use them mindfully.

The words we speak have a way of impacting and shaping the reality in which we live and the way we perceive the world, including ourselves.

1) I am complete vibration ~ I flow with ease

2) I am source energy ~ limitless

3) I am that I am ~ everything that I say I am

4) I am the way maker ~ as so I thinketh

5) I am intentionally & wonderfully made ~ I lack nothing

6) I am the knowledge that I seek ~ greatness lives in me, my knowledge is power

"Just Keep Blooming"

SIERRA CLARK

has had the gift of being someone people can talk to as far back as she can remember. She's been the voice of reason for many, and it seems even at a young age, people valued her two cents.

In 41 years, she's never met a stranger. Yep, she's the person random people find comfort in talking to in the line at the grocery store.

Is it her laughter that's calming and explosive all at the same time? Perhaps it's her magnetic personality that draws you in like your favorite movie. Could it be her illuminating smile that feels like sunshine? Or the warmth of her soul that comforts you like a slice of grandma's warm apple pie?

Some might say she's a beacon or even call it a gift. Either way there is no question as to why she's been invited to speak in pool pits around her city. She finds great joy in mentoring at a few local high schools and elementary schools.

There is no reason to wonder why, when doing speaking engagements, she connects with the audience. Whether if it's at a women's retreat with a room of 500+ women or something more intimate like in a local park with a small group of people.

Whatever it is, you can expect Sierra to do it with T. L. C while connecting with you. She takes that saying, "Put yourself, in my shoes," literally.

Sierra finds joy in doing unto others as she would do unto herself. So, she delivers as if she too was sitting in the audience and needed the message herself.

CONTACT SIERRA:

✉ INFO@SIERRACLARK.LIFE

🌐 SIERRACLARK.LIFE